QUADERNI DEL DIPARTIMENTO DI GIURI
DELL'UNIVERSITÀ DI TORINO

11/2019

EPISTEMIC COMMUNITIES AT THE BOUNDARIES OF LAW: CLINICS AS A PARADIGM IN THE REVOLUTION OF LEGAL EDUCATION IN THE EUROPEAN MEDITERRANEAN CONTEXT

EDITED BY
CECILIA BLENGINO AND ANDRÉS GASCÓN-CUENCA

Ledizioni

Opera finanziata con il contributo del Dipartimento di Giurisprudenza dell'Università di Torino.

Il presente volume è stato preliminarmente sottoposto a un processo di referaggio anonimo, nel rispetto dell'anonimato sia dell'Autore sia dei revisori (double blind peer review). La valutazione è stata affidata a due esperti del tema trattato, designati dal Direttore del Dipartimento di Giurisprudenza dell'Università di Torino.
Entrambi i revisori hanno formulato un giudizio positivo sull'opportunità di pubblicare il presente volume".

Via Alamanni, 11 – 20141 Milano – Italy
www.ledizioni.it
info@ledizioni.it

Cecilia Blengino and Andrés Gascón-Cuenca (edited by), *Epistemic Communities at the Boundaries of Law: Clinics as a Paradigm in the Revolution of Legal Education in the European Mediterranean Context*

Prima edizione: aprile 2019
ISBN 9788855260046

Progetto grafico: ufficio grafico Ledizioni

Informazioni sul catalogo e sulle ristampe dell'editore: www.ledizioni.it

Indice

Preface

Catherine F. Klein[*]

I begin with a few quotes from two of the educational theorists I keep close to my heart.

> "There's no such thing as neutral education. Education either functions as an instrument to bring about conformity or freedom."
> Paulo Freire, *Pedagogy of the Oppressed*

> "Liberation is a praxis: the action and reflection of men and women upon their world in order to transform it."
> Paulo Freire, *Pedagogy of the Oppressed*

> "Give the pupils something to do, not something to learn; and the doing is of such a nature as to demand thinking; learning naturally results."
> John Dewey, *Democracy and Education*

> "If we teach today's students as we taught yesterday's, we rob them of tomorrow."
> John Dewey, *Democracy and Education*

For a long time, educational theorists such as Paulo Freire and John Dewey have been telling us that engaging learners in real problems in the real world is the best way to stimulate and enhance learning. Clinical legal education is a movement that first ignited in the United States forty-five years ago, and has been incrementally taking hold in Europe and the rest of the world. Clinics are in part a response to theorists like Freire and Dewey,

[*] Professor of Law and Director of the Columbus Community Legal Services. The Catholic University of America. United States of America.

and others, who have urged us to rethink radically the goals and methods of education, and to re-envision the role that our universities play in our societies.

I have participated in, as well as observed, the development of legal clinics in a number of countries in Europe, including Poland, Spain and Italy, for some time with the greatest of interest and appreciation. For some time, Continental Western Europe seemed to resist (or at least ignore) the development of clinics. However, this picture is changing rapidly in dynamic and creative ways. European universities are creating legal clinics in great numbers today. This book focuses primarily on Spanish and Italian universities, and the exciting clinical experiments and programs that are becoming an important part of their curricula, educating the next generation of lawyers in critically important ways. These university-based clinics expose law students and lawyers to the devastating injustices —large and small— that exist in their communities. Students learn important lessons that most of them will never forget, and that they will carry forward with them into practice. To do clinical work, students engage and apply substantive knowledge, and learn the professional and interpersonal skills and values that will enable them to engage in the work of a lawyer in an effective, value-driven way.

Collaboration and teamwork are hallmarks of clinical education. Many faculty members with years of classroom teaching experience comment on how much they enjoy the more personal contact with students in the clinic and the opportunity to work side-by-side with students as they learn how to solve problems for themselves. The process that lead to the creation of this book clearly reflects this value. The various authors have worked together, participated in educational exchanges, and shared teaching materials and ideas. The research and scholarship displayed in this book is a result of this synergy. Their shared experience, insight, reflection, and wisdom will benefit the entire clinical education community.

In addition, other networks have also helped to foster this work. For the past 20 years, The Global Alliance for Justice Education (GAJE), an organization of law teachers and others committed to achieving justice through education, has focused on the promotion and support of socially relevant legal education. More recently, the European Network of Clinical Legal Education (ENCLE) has also fostered relationships and sharing of ideas and research about clinics. Through these networks and others, the authors of this book have participated in workshops and conferences with other like-minded law professors from many different countries. This exchange has undoubtedly contributed to the creation of the ideas expressed in this book. Often at such conferences, participants are encouraged to imagine a law school whose primary mission is to reduce injustice in society. What would it look like? How would professors in such a school teach? What would students do? The authors are grappling with these big picture questions in the context of their own institutions and clinics.

As richly described in the various chapters of this book, we see that clinics can act as a window to the functioning of law and the legal system. Clinics allow students and faculty to see how laws and the legal system are functioning for groups of people who otherwise likely would not be a part of the common experience of professors and their students: poor people generally, migrants and refugees, women and children exploited by trafficking, people with disabilities, ethnic minorities, prisoners, and so on. Legal systems the world over tend to give less care and attention to the problems of the poor and other disempowered groups, and such people usually lack access to well-educated legal advocates to help them fight to make the legal system work for them. Through clinic cases, students and faculty see the day-to-day lives of people marginalized by the society, see how the law affects and influences their lives, and see how it serves or fails to serve them. For law professors involved in clinical education, such as the authors of this book, heightened awareness of the law's operation for poor people adds another important perspective to the subjects of their research and work as commentators on the law. Students can also be inspired to select topics for research papers, master or PhD theses by exposure to problems in the law and legal system as it functions for their clients.

In thinking about the social justice goals of clinical education, it may be useful to refer to the principles enumerated in the conference report from the GAJE Second Worldwide Conference in Durban, South Africa. Participants identified some critical elements of justice education. The Spanish and Italian clinics portrayed in this book embrace and reflect many of these principles:

- Justice education is a systematic approach that involves social, political and historical awareness; there may be no universal 'curriculum' for justice education, but there are some principles: promoting equality among all peoples, providing access to information and the legal services that enforce rights, supporting the need for value information, demonstrating inclusiveness and not just tolerance of diversity, encouraging social responsibility from students and academic staff.
- Justice education seeks to identify the values underlying law, taking into consideration different national and ethnic backgrounds, religions, and cultures.
- Justice education develops the notion that acceptance of responsibilities is of equal importance as the assertion of rights.
- Justice education follows a practical, participatory, and action/reflection learning approach to develop tools for shifting power balances.

- Justice education is self-reflective and self-critical; students are taught to use critical reflection techniques to link law and experience in their work.
- Justice education is inclusive, thereby modeling the giving up of power, reserving judgment, and showing empathy. Non-lawyer actors in the legal process participate in and learn from justice education; clients are invited to talk to students about their experiences with the legal system.
- Justice education relies on innovative, convinced, and inspiring teachers who see fairness and due process as basic in their mentoring (teaching by example and within communities). Justice education teachers are dedicated to helping others involved in law/legal education to think more broadly.
- Justice education should be the true focus of legal/lawyer education; law school education is only a part of this greater whole (and gives no guarantee of justice *per se*).

As the European clinics grow in number and in strength, they will have an ever larger impact on the students, clients, attorneys and professors involved. Clinics offer valuable opportunities for faculty and students together, often in cooperation with practitioners, to make the aspirations expressed in university mission statements a reality. The goal of this book is to assist and support organizing new clinics, as well as strengthen those that already exist. The book is also an example of professors reporting, analyzing and reflecting on their programs with the goal of continually improving them. In my view, the publication of this book is unquestioningly a constructive step toward strengthening clinical education in Europe and the rest of the world. I am confident readers will enjoy and appreciate the authors' contributions to this book as much as I have. This book provides inspiring examples of how we can work together to further the revolution in legal education.

"Should you sit upon a cloud you would not see the boundary line between one country and another, nor the boundary stone between a farm and a farm. It is a pity you cannot sit upon a cloud"

(K. Gibran, Sand and Foam, 1926)

CECILIA BLENGINO[1] AND ANDRÉS GASCÓN-CUENCA[2]

Legal Clinics as a Paradigm in the Revolution of Legal Education in the European Mediterranean Context

Introduction

The present collaborative volume is the result of the fortunate circumstances and synergies that had placed its curators in an alike starting situation when it comes to the reflection on clinical legal education: firstly, a joining legal philosophical background; secondly, the fact of belonging to countries, Italy and Spain, that pertain to the legal culture of civil law of the continental Europe; thirdly, a consolidated experience in legal clinical teaching oriented to overcome the formative model of legal positivism that still today characterizes our legal university degrees; fourthly, being highly active in the development of the global movement of legal clinics by participating and organizing conferences in both the international and European networks of clinical legal education; and finally, creating, reflecting and developing together many projects that formulate the spirit of the epistemic community promoted by the legal clinic colleagues.

Accordingly, being these premises the scaffolding of our work, we felt the need to urgently rethink about the role played today by the legal clinics in the

1 Cecilia Blengino: Università degli Studi di Torino, Dipartimento di Giurisprudenza (Italy). Assistant Professor of Sociology of Law.

2 Andrés Gascón-Cuenca: Human Rights Institute. University of Valencia (Spain). Postdoctoral researcher. Generalitat Valenciana APOSTD/2017/093. Member of the research project: Transformaciones de la justicia. Autonomía, inequidad y ejercicio de derechos (DER2016-78356-P).

European Mediterranean context, in which we live, teach, research and act.

Clinical Legal Education (CLE) represents a revolutionary methodology of teaching and learning Law that, as we will see in the following chapters, is rising in a particularly difficult time. It is developing its influence in a moment where cultural and political borders, with visible and veiled actions, are today stressing and pushing the Law in a direction that redefines, limits, and empties of content core human rights. Thus, this situation evidences, on one hand, the inadequacy of basing the teaching and the learning of the Law in a pure positivism model, as it does not provide an adequate answer to face this involution in the protection of rights, and on the other hand, the need of developing law students' critical thinking.

This book is one of the outcomes resulting from some of the reflections that emerged during a period of faculty exchange and research that allowed us to work together for a few months in Turin and to involve our colleagues and friends with whom for some time we are sharing the interest and commitment for application of clinical methodology in many critical areas of law[3].

Thus, analyzing the current social, economic, political and cultural situation, it inevitably leaded us to confront ourselves with the dramatic situation we are experiencing at the European level, with increasing limitations and barriers to the full respect, and even to the recognition, of most basic human rights. The restriction on the exercise of rights for vulnerable persons is clearly promoted by creating physical borders and juridical limitations with which the recognition of rights is refused to many people, for instance, migrants trying to enter in Europe. These differences between those who are recognized as rights bearers and the ones who are excluded, are a daily reality in juridical practices that take place in a general and structural context of exclusion against those pointed out as foes, mainly migrants, *poor people*, and prisoners.

Given this reality, in this book we highlight the crucial role that legal clinics play in confronting this situation. The paradigm of legal clinical education requires us to think about legal clinics as social, cultural and political actors that face the challenges posed by the boundaries of the law, trying to force them in order to construct a more inclusive society, not only regarding cultural aspects but also in fomenting an extended interpretation of the contents of the rights.

So that, in these brief introductory pages we will explain the essential lines of reasoning that leaded us to think about legal clinics as communi-

---

3 From march and july 2018 Andrés Gascon Cuenca has been in Turin as a visiting researcher at the Department of Law, partecipating to a research program lead by Claudio Sarzotti and Cecilia Blengino. A first chance for discussing reflections among colleagues was the workshop "Epistemic communities at the boundaries of law: some reflections about the Development of the Mediterranean Legal Clinic Model" held on 11 May at the University of Turin.

ties of practice placed at the borders of the rights recognition system of the legal orders. Precisely, in the following pages we will research into this reality by analyzing the different roles that the clinical experience has with the contribution of some colleagues, experts in CLE. This task will be generally performed by, firstly, introducing new ways of juridical action hitherto unpublished in civil law systems, secondly, enriching the formation of the jurist with the fundamental contribution of empirical research, and finally, by promoting actively the access to the rights and justice of people placed in a vulnerable situation.

After years of impermeability (Wilson, 2009), the Mediterranean Europe has been recently reached by the innovative rise of the global clinical movement (Bloch, 2011; Wilson 2017). This continental European clinical movement – which started in Spain in the 2000s, and was followed, a few years later, in Italy – presents some original characteristics.

The development of legal clinics represents radical change towards the dominant model of legal education in the Continental Europe. In that context, the current educational model derives from the primacy of law and its non-political nature, veiling and marginalizing any understanding of existing gaps between the law and the legal codes, as well as the living relationship within positive law, power, control and society. Thus, the innovative wave of the clinical movement, even in the EU civil law educational systems, introduces a revolution in the way professors teach law that shakes many of the cornerstones in which the traditional methodologies of teaching of law are based, mainly, legal positivism ones. The primacy of the study of law using codes, the utilization of the exegetical methodology when lecturing, the historical diffidence towards a practical dimension of education, the humanities and interdisciplinarity (Vogliotti, 2018), are the premises challenged by the clinical methodology (Blengino, 2018, p. 210). Therefore, the innovative impact of the legal clinics towards the traditional methodologies for teaching and study Law has contributed to shake the capacities of the educational system up, by reshaping the ideas of Law and Legal knowledge themselves, to actually have a crux role in the change of positive law.

Consequently, CLE rethinks not only the methodologies, but foremost the objectives and purposes of legal education. The *learning by doing* methodology adopted by CLE overcomes the old dogmatic approach that supports the idea that legal education should transmit just the technical knowledge of law by studying the codes. CLE encourages the idea of rising awareness in future lawyers about the breaks and gaps that separate the realities of the law in action, from law in the books (Frank, 1933; Kruse, 2011-2012; Perelman, 2014). So that, it challenges the established ideas of juridical knowledge formed within the modern paradigm of law, and also the Kelsenean representation of law as a system endowed with its own internal coherence. To this idea CLE opposes an anti-formalist conception of the normative system that allows us to underline its interdependence of with other orders (Vogliotti, 2014).

In such a way, the boundaries on the formation of the lawyers expand themselves – in a new way for the European legal curricula – towards an interdisciplinary approach, a reflexive practice, a development of critical thinking and to the empirical research on law. While traditional EU civil models support the concept of neutrality and the non-political nature of law, CLE allows us to grasp the relationship between positive law and power that is realized in law in context (Bailleux & Ost, 2013). Assuming a bottom-up perspective, the "thinking by case" methodology and the "ascending alchemy" (Perelman, 2014, p.113) through which the clinics approach the law lead to an epistemological renewal of the research on law and open new frontiers of it.

As a consequence, the lecture of the Law and the boundaries between teaching and learning it are severely modified by CLE. In the new bottom-up learning process, the traditional monopoly of the lecturer on the process of teaching law, in fact, disappears. Top-down teaching is replaced by a bottom-up procedure in which teachers and students are continuously and interactively working together to understand the contradictions of the law in context, and to identify the precise factors that hinder the access to the justice in order to give and appropriate answer to legal problems. In this process, professors are required to introduce new teaching methodologies that develop this bottom-up process. So that, it constitutes a special epistemic community of legal clinicians. It progresses through a continuous and reciprocal exchange of knowledge and expertise within it, as it is composed by academics, professionals, students and other social activists who operate in different legal systems.

Therefore, according to our vision, legal clinics can adopt many layouts, from a live client clinic, international human right clinic, penitentiary law clinic, and many others. But all of them share the same scope, developing projects related to social justice that have an impact on the society where the clinic is located (Gascón-Cuenca, 2016). So that, when developing our work, we are required to identify the areas the Law does not reach and the people it leaves out in the cold, in order to step in and assist them, as they are placed in a situation of vulnerability by the system itself. This situation can be the result of many factors, but regularly, we find behind of the scheme of the case, patterns of structural discrimination that expel from the system certain groups of population (Gascón-Cuenca, 2018). Thus, this is a unique opportunity for professors to teach students, not only about the relevant role that the law has as a transformative mean in the society (García-Añón, 2013), but also the need for protecting and guaranteeing human rights. These topics are barley taught through the degree in law, so it is our obligation as clinical professors to unveil these relations of power, in order to fight for a more progressive and rights-based society. By having this approach, we empower and recognize the importance the students have as dynamic actors within the jurisdictional system, as future legal operators.

Additionally, it should be noted that the development of the legal clinical movement also emphasized the dissolution of the traditional boundaries of the law in another sense. It is the transnationalization of legal practices, in which the distance between the principles of common law and civil law is fading away, and where there is a mutual exchange of ideas and practices coming from different legal systems. The originality of the clinics at the epistemological level, manifests itself both globally and locally. The transnationalism of clinical legal education comes through the international networks that constitute the main references of the community of clinicians. The meetings of the GAJE and the ENCLE networks represent crucial opportunities for constantly learning about clinical methodology and exchanging experiences.

In this sense, the grow of legal clinics in Mediterranean context can be seen as an example of how the transnational circulation of legal models influences every aspect of the law, including structures of legal expertise and Education (Barbera, 2018, p.64). Therefore, the development of the legal clinical movement in this Mediterranean area is an evident outcome of a 'boundary of boundaries' and of a cultural exchange between the legal clinical tradition of North American origin and endogenous factors. So that, the epistemic community of legal clinicians is indubitably a transnational phenomenon, through which the exportation of US clinical legal methodologies – i. e. reflective practice – meet the specificities of each regional and local contexts, enriching itself of new elements and ideas. As a consequence, the origins and developments of the clinical movement in the Mediterranean European area, present some characterizing traits.

As argued by Richard Wilson, the spread of clinical legal education has not to be considered as a US "clinical imperialism", but as an element of "development policy" (Wilson, 2011, p.143). Unlike what has happened in other realities, such as in Eastern Europe, the process of developing the legal clinical methodologies in the European Mediterranean area has been a substantially spontaneous process. This is based on a combination of shared political and cultural factors: the growing dissatisfaction of teachers with a sound *law and society* towards the dogmatic approach of legal teaching (Blengino, 2018), the cultural legacy and the resumption of the reflections and proposals advanced in Italy since the '70s by the movement for access to justice (Cappelletti, 1979), and the awareness about the increasing spaces of ineffectiveness of rights.

Particularly, the influence of this last scholar explains why the clinical development in the Mediterranean area is oriented from the very beginning towards objectives of access to justice and, specifically, giving priority to the objective of combating the *legal poverty*, by working lively on context of social deprivation (prisons, migrations...). Moreover, having in mind that, often, these areas fall outside of both the interest of traditional academic lecturing and the attention of the institutions. Where access to justice and respect for human rights becomes more difficult, the legal clinics step in to embrace the legacy of the demands of Cappelletti and Barth.

Contents

Benefitting from the synergies created by the large faculty community that has embrace CLE as a way of teaching and learning Law, the Mediterranean legal clinical movement is experiencing a fruitful expansion in the last years in our continent. Not only the quantity of legal clinics joining the European Network of Clinical Legal Education (ENCLE) is on the rise, but also the number of delegates participating at its conferences with high-quality presentations. We have made direct experience of the growth and development of the European clinical community, being our workteams[4] actively enrolled in the promotion of the European CLE network. We have energetically worked together in joining projects, exchanging faculty, and presenting the results of their researchers during ENCLE conferences, such as the 4th ENCLE conference organized in 2016 in Valencia, and the 6th one organized in 2018 in Turin.

Thus, the same scenario is the one we can find at the global level, if we look at the past conferences organized by the Global Alliance for Justice Education (GAJE). The Legal Clinic for Social Justice and the Human Rights Institute of the University of Valencia organized in 2011 the 6th GAJE conference altogether with 9th International Journal of Legal Clinical Education Conference (IJCLE). In 2015 and in 2017, members of our clinical teams attended in the 8th and the 9th GAJE Conference held respectively in Eskisehir (Turkey) and Puebla (Mexico), presenting the results of a joining project aimed to enhance the results legal clinics have in terms of the impact of their work in their local communities.

Consequently, this book is a reality that directly benefits from both the active exchange of expertise just mentioned, and the shared reflections about

---

4 The Legal Clinic for Social Justice of the University of Valencia, the Legal Clinic Prison and Rights I and the Human Trafficking of the University of Turin.

how we understand CLE. The following chapters gather together the results of our ongoing projects. Now we are on a crux time for the development of CLE in the European context that has as a cornerstone the need of bringing a new paradigm into the legal studies.

In such a current context, as the one we have in Italy and Spain, the clinical movement can be understood as a new actor placed at the border of the traditional system, that takes a position in the single communities of practice (Wegner, 2014) in which the process of learning, interpreting and action takes place. It moves away from the rigidity of academic roles, to the collaboration and the exchange of experiences, competences and knowledge among law professors, students, lawyers, NGOs, and other social and institutional actors. We, all united by the common aim of using reflective methodologies as ways to overcome the gaps in the injustices of our legal systems.

Thus, this volume is divided in two different areas. In the first one, contributions research into some general questions regarding the revolution introduced by this new paradigm introduced by CLE in the Law studies and in the continental legal system. The following section looks into two spheres that represent sections of the Law that are *closed* and placed at the limits of the rights-based legal system, so a critical area for legal clinics to work and collaborate. For this aim, colleagues analyze and present some successful projects developed in the field of penitentiary, and migration law. Succinctly, when it comes to the first part:

Cecilia Blengino focuses on the socio-legal epistemology introduced by CLE in the European continental law faculties. Her chapter enhances instruments of reflective practice, while presenting clinics through the educational paradigm of communities of practice, underlying the crucial role played by the cooperation among academics, students, NGOs, lawyers and other social actors in both the learning and research processes.

Andrés Gascón-Cuenca researches into the specific characteristics present in Spain and Italy when it comes to CLE as nations that have a similar welfare state model, severally hit by the 2008 economic crisis. This context of necessity has been used as an excuse to curtail some fundamental rights, and it has had an immediate impact on the life of people, especially on those placed in a situation of vulnerability by the legal system. Thus, this contribution particularly focuses in the characteristics present at the time legal clinics aroused in these countries, as a way to identify, on one hand, the social needs and, on the other hand, the project challenges we faced and we still facing when developing our work.

José García-Añón focuses on the role of the "other actors" (NGOs, universities and legal clinics) as complements to other pro bono activities. It explores not only their impact on court decisions, but also in building the law or the case law, as part of the right of access to justice, i.e., their role in the construction of legal legitimacy. This piece of research takes a broad perspective on justice incorporating distributive, retributive, and restorative dimensions. This analysis is done through answering the *who, how,* and *what* questions regarding the idea of justice. This approach implies a change in the role that the various actors involved in legal disputes, standards of justice, and forms of access to justice have.

Jose A. García-Sáez explores the potential of legal clinics as a teaching methodology in the degree of law. He focuses his chapter on the subjects of human rights and criminal law. Starting with a general contextualization, he continues underlining some skills and values that students can develop through the clinical methodology. Moreover, he also reflects about the importance clinics should have within the curriculum of law, and empha-sizes strategic litigation as a mean for transferring knowledge to society.

When it comes to the second part:

Silvia Mondino looks into the role that CLE can play in the peniten-tiary system. She reflects on an experience of community lawyering clinic in prison. She focuses on the type of community with which the clinic she collaborates with interacts, the prisoners, and highlighting its characteris-tics and complexities. She emphasizes how the development of this CLE project creates a particular community, with specific dynamics of function-ing, composed of students and prisoners, who work together to ensure the achievement of a common purpose. This learning environment is paramount in the development of the project, with low-structured situations in which students, benefiting from their work with their peers, can experience new challenges that stimulate their cognitive resources. Moreover, she stresses out that a specific attention to the learning method also helps to define in a more precise way useful activities to ensure the empowerment of prisoners in exercising their own rights and, to develop original paths of research.

Claudio Sarzotti investigates also about prison, but from a different per-spective. His contribution focuses on the specific aim that makes him to feel necessary leading students to approach the prison system. He proposes carceral tours as an useful tool for students to understand the complexity of the prison system but also to improve their awareness and memory about the ways in which our penal system has been constructed over time.

With regards to the relation between CLE, human rights and migration, Maurizio Veglio, researches into what he identifies as *theatres of humiliation of human dignity*, the migrants' detention centers. Facilities where the suffer has been legalized and institutionalized, so that are a must-field for legal clinics. His chapter reports the joint and concentric effort that lead clini-cal students, lawyers, NGOs and lecturers to reveal how segregation affects fundamental rights of detainees: freedom, well-being, dignity, safety. Legal clinics therefore transform the very essence of academic research into an investigation on crime and punishment of non-citizens.

Ulrich Stege focuses in the recent European fluxes of migration. Thus, in the last years, the movement of persons passing across borders has been a cause for major political and legal debates and struggle. At the same time, CLE has developed enormously in many parts of Europe and Africa. With a special focus on law clinics working for the benefit of migrants and asylum seekers, his chapter looks into the CLE movement on both sides of the Mediterranean Sea and identifies what motivates and influences clinicians from both continents to engage with justice education in the support of migrants and refugees. After a brief description of the migration context and a quick overview of the CLE movement in Europe and in Africa, the chapter investigates some very specific CLE models from both continents in order to gain a better picture about some interesting strategies and motivations aiming at "crossing borders and boundaries" of legal education and the law.

---

* This introductive chapter is the fully result of shared reflections between the editors of this volume. Nevertheless, for organizing purposes Cecilia Blengino wrote the first section (Introduction) and Andrés Gascon Cuenca wrote the second one (Contents).

References

Bailleux A. (2018), Quelle formation pour quel juriste et quel droit? Libération et responsabilisation de l'étudiant bruxellois, in M. Vogliotti, *Pour une nouvelle éducation juridique,* L'Harmattan, Paris, p. 167- 193

Bailleux A., F. Ost (2013), "Droit, contexte et interdisciplinaritè: refondation d'une demarche", in *Revue interdisciplinaire d'études juridiques,* 1 (70), p. 25 – 44.

Barbera M. (2018), The Emergence of an Italian Clinical Legal Education. Movement: the University of Brescia Law Clinic, in A. Alemanno and L. Khadar (ed), *Reinventing Legal Education How Clinical Education is Reforming the Teaching and Practice of Law in Europe,* Cambridge

University Press, p. 59-75.

Blengino C. (2018), "Interdisciplinarity and Clinical Legal Education: how synergies can improve access to rights in prison", in *International Journal of Clinical Legal Education*, 25, 1, p. 210- 239.

Bloch, F. S., ed. (2011). *The global clinical movement. Educating lawyers to social justice*, Oxford University Press.

Cappelletti, M. (1979). "Accesso alla giustizia: conclusione di un progetto internazionale di ricerca giuridico-sociologica", in *Foro Italiano*, 54, p.54-61.

Kruse, K. (2011-2012). "Getting Real About Legal Realism, New Legal Realism and Clinical Legal Education", in *New York Law School Law Review*, Vol. 56.

Perelman, J. (2014). "Penser la pratique, théoriser le droit en action: des cliniques juridiques et des nouvelles frontières épistémologiques du droit". In *Revue interdisciplinaire d'études juridiques* 72 (2), p. 133-153.

Vogliotti M. (2014), La fine del grande stile, in V. Barsotti (ed), *L'identità delle scienze giuridiche in ordinamenti multilivello. Quaderni del dottorato fiorentino in scienze giuridiche*, Maggioli, Firenze.

Vogliotti M. (2018), *Pour une nouvelle éducation juridique,* L'Harmattan, Paris.

Wilson, R. (2009). *Western Europe: Last Holdout in the Worldwide Acceptance of Clinical Legal Education*, German Law Journal 10, 7, p. 823-846.

Wilson, R. (2011). *Beyond legal imperialism. US Clinical Legal Education and the New Law and Development*, in F. Bloch (ed) *The Global Clinical Movement: Educating Lawyers for Social Justice*, Oxford University Press, p.135-150.

Wilson R. (2017), *The Global Evolution of Clinical Legal Education. More than a Method.* Cambridge University Press.

Cecilia Blengino[1]

Clinical Legal Education and Reflective Practice: The Epistemology of Practice on the Boundaries of Law

Introduction

Amongst the new ideas introduced by the spread of Clinical Legal Education (CLE) in the civil law European juridical systems, this essay focuses primarily on the paradigm shift brought about by the CLE – rather than on methods of juridical education – on the notions of law and juridical research, which have consolidated in over two centuries in the framework of the modern European juridical paradigm. The socio legal epistemology introduced by CLE is explored respectively focusing on reflective practice as innovative tool in legal education and considering legal clinics through the educational paradigm of the community of practice.

The Role of Legal Clinics in XXI Century European Universities

After years of being impermeable to the innovative wave of CLE (Wilson, 2009; Bloch, 2011), the clinical development process can be considered fully under way also in the context of continental Western Europe (Wilson, 2017, p. 301 ss)[2]. The maturity of the clinical experiences is today finally starting

---

1 Dipartimento di Giurisprudenza, Università degli studi di Torino.

2 The most recent recognition of the Italian clinics refers in 2015 to the existence of 14 clinics and to 7 being set up (Bartoli, 2015). Although there are no updated official data, this number is today certainly increased. In Spain, the network of

to align with the development, by those who practice clinical teaching, of a reflection empirically based on the innovative nature of the clinical model.

The revolutionary capacity of CLE may be examined in the viewpoint of Jeremy Perelman's interrogatives: «*Quelle formation et quelle recherche pour quels droits et quels juristes ?*» (2014, p. 133).

The answers provided by CLE to these four questions differ radically from those of the approach deriving from legal positivism, which still predominates in the faculties of Law in continental Europe.

The roots of the paradigm shift[3] triggered by legal clinics at the level of education go back to the ability of the clinics, as already highlighted by the American legal realists (Frank, 1933; Llewellyn, 1935), to oppose a dogmatic and artificial attitude towards law education, to enable students to understand and to fill in the gaps and contradictions between law in books and law in action by means of the interaction of the law practice with society and everyday life (Blengino, 2018a, p.210).

These characteristics and objectives acquire further significance and potential in the context of continental Europe[4].

Adopting law in action as a subject of teaching overturns the notion of Law established by legal positivism. The educational model resulting from the primacy of statute law and from an interpretation of law based on the logical deductive reasoning has led to an acritical, dogmatic model of jurist (Blázquez, 2011). The exegetical methodology brings together both the interpretation and teaching of law in a non-problematic transmission of norms and principles crystallized in timeless categories (Vogliotti, 2014, p.

Spanish clinics includes 19 legal clinics in 2017 (http://diarium.usal.es/clinicajuridica/red-universitaria-de-clinicas-juridicas-espanolas/).

3   The epistemological concept of paradigm is used here in the meaning of T. Khun, which is referred to in order to indicate those theoretical models, accepted as tools of knowledge within the scientific communities, which enable communication among community members . Such models remain valid until the point where problems manage to find a solution within their epistemological framework. When this heuristic ability is reduced, the paradigms in use are replaced "per saltum" by new ones (Khun, 1970).

4   A review of the clinical experience of the French university of Sciences Po is offered by Perelman (2014). Some reflections about clinics in the context of civil law tradition and European clinical culture have been proposed by Poillot (2014, 2016). Regarding the evolution of clinical legal education in Spain reference should be made, among others, to Blázquez-Martín (2010), García-Añón (2013), Gascón-Cuenca (2016) and Fernandez-Artiach et al (2017). A recent reflection on the specifics of the movement and the clinical methodology in the civil law area is given by Amato (2017) and Barbera (2018). A first volume collecting the experiences of the Italian clinical network as well as theoretical considerations by Italian clinical teachers is represented by Maestroni, Brambilla and Carrer (2018).

166 ; ID, 2018). Moreover, the affirmation of law as a self-contained technical subject has lent support to the concept of its neutrality and its non-political nature. When teaching is limited to transfer normative contents, it ends up concealing the ideological dimension of law and it tends to reproduce the power structures and inequalities existing in society (Kennedy, 2004, p. 591). That is also true for the area of learning, since the relationship between those who possess and transfer dogmatic knowledge and those who receive it presupposes and attributes power to the first.

These elements, together with the growing tendency towards professionalization and competition, are the key elements of the crisis of the university in the XXI century as a place of education of critical thinking (De Sousa Santos, 2012; ID., 2016).

It's necessary to be aware that the calls for change arising from the Bologna Process[5] include, simultaneously, fertile ground for the legal clinics, but also significant aspects of ambiguity which might affect the roots of the innovative potential of such educational tool.

In this scenario, it is important to stress that legal clinics are not just a way of introducing practice to the juridical study careers, while keeping substantially unchanged the theoretical presuppositions of juridical formalism (Blengino, 2018a). The clinical experience must be considered rather as a socio-juridical epistemology of law in action, where resolving the separation of theory from practice represents the consequence of a conception of law as a *phenomenon which is revealed through practice* (Perelman, 2014, p. 133 ff.; Brooks & Madden, 2011-12).

CLE should be considered as a space-time of active learning: the training is designed and planned in students' legal experience to enable them to take responsibility for their learning, through a process of reflection on the process itself (Garcia Anon, 2014, p. 158).

The *ascending alchemy* (Perelman, 2014) produced by legal clinics therefore introduces radical innovation to legal education in continental Europe: the chance to debate the supposed neutrality of law; the ability to identify the social, economic and cultural variables, which impede full effectiveness of the laws; recognition of interdisciplinarity; the call to intervene with concrete action to improve access to justice and remove the obstacles preventing formal laws from being translated into laws in action.

Working upwards from the concrete to the abstract, the clinic overturns

---

5 The Bologna Process is an intergovernmental cooperation of 48 European countries, started in 1999 with the aim to create a cohesive higher education zone. It guides "the collective effort to support the modernisation of education and training system to make sure these meet the needs of a changing labour market" (http://ec.europa.eu/education/policy/higher-education/bologna-process_en).

the viewpoint of the dogmatic approach to law and abandons the exegetic method (Carnelutti, 1935, p. 173). The most radical epistemological revolution brought by legal clinics into education within the European framework of civil law consists of their choosing the law in context as subject and aim of learning, focusing on the relationships between law and its environment as a central element of understanding the juridical phenomenon (Bailleux – Ost, 2013, p. 35). As observed by Kruse, "in the heart of law in action […] students daily encounter the gaps between what the law says, what it aspires to be, and what legal officials actually do, and are therefore poised to engage questions about the role of law in society" (2011-2012, p. 317-318).

Whitin the Medirreanean European context, the interest and the awareness of the potential that clinical legal education offers in combining a practical approach with theoretical considerations, research, education and action has been present in the development from the outset (Marella & Rigo, 2015; Barbera, 2018; Blengino, 2018b; Asta et al 2018; Alaimo et al 2018). Being aware that the clinics constitute a special observatory on law in action, various research projects have been developed within them. These include, among others: observatories on the situation of migrant detention centers[6]; an observatory aimed at collecting and analyzing the decisions concerning detention and expulsion of third-country nationals by Justices of the Peace (Giudice di Pace) on Italian national territory[7]; an observatory on exploitation of labour and gangmasters in the agricultural areas of Southern Italy[8]; empirical research on problematical profiles related to the management of asylum procedures in Sicily[9]; a research project on procedures and processes of identification of victims of human trafficking among asylum seekers[10].

---

6   See for example the report "Betwixt and Between: Turin's CIE. A human rights investigation into Turin's immigration detention centre" (http://ideas.iuctorino.it/RePEc/iuc-rpa-per/1-12_Betwixt-and-Between-1.pdf) realized in 2012 by the HRML Clinic and the report realized by a team of Spanish legal clinics focusing on several detention centres in Spain (https://ojs.uv.es/index.php/clinicajuridica/article/view/6472/6264.

7   The mentioned project has been developed and carried out by the legal clinics of Rome III and by the HRML clinic of the International University College of Turin.

8   Research sponsored by the legal clinic of the University of Rome III and by the student association Di.FRO (acronym of Diritti di Frontiera, that means *rights at the borders* (Asta et al, 2018).

9   Research carried out by the legal clinic of Palermo on human rights, described by Alaimo *et al*, 2018.

10   This is the project called "Against Human Trafficking: innovative strategies against human trafficking in Piedmont", developed by the anti-human trafficking legal clinic of the Department of Law of the University of Turin and the International University College.

By placing the search for sources of knowledge of law in action under direct observation (Kruse, 2011-2012, p. 317) the legal clinics allow candidate legal experts to experiment with the idea that law is not an orderly system of verbal formulae, but rather a disorderly world of interpretations and procedures. The "vivid sense of the existence of breaks, gaps, and problems" (Frank, 1933, p. 920), which is a consequence of the empirical observation of the juridical phenomenon carried out by the legal clinics, also makes it possible to recognize the essence of law as an instrument for regulating power relationships and to observe to what extent, on the level of social experience, the exercise of rights depends on the positions of power in which the subjects find themselves in relation to one another (Tomeo, 2013, p. 38).

While this awareness in the USA made the clinics a tool for the activism of Critical Legal Studies (Kennedy, 1982), in the continental European context, the awareness of the disparity in the distribution of power, both in imposing interpretation on the law and in having access to the law, binds the legal clinics to the Movement for Access to Justice (Cappelletti 1979 & 1981). Legal clinics fully acknowledge the calls of Mauro Cappelletti to understand the inadequacies of the rigid apparatus of formal justice in responding to unequal opportunities in terms of access to rights, as well as to intervene with new solutions to overcome economic, social and cultural impediments that prevented certain people from fully enjoying their rights.

Since structures and contents of the clinics are influenced by the concrete contexts in which local juridical practice takes form (Bloch, 2008, p. 114), it is easy to understand why the first clinical experiments in the countries of Mediterranean Europe were directed from the outset towards the social justice mission, involving themselves mainly in human rights and social rights and focusing on support for vulnerable persons, such as immigrants, asylum seekers, detainees.

Lastly, clinical legal education radically widens the spaces of interdisciplinarity, i.e. a significant sharing of knowledge and skills, leading the activities of teaching and learning to converge on a common aim (Tokarz, 2006).

While the separation of the disciplines leaves people incapable of capturing the entirety, the process of knowledge driven by problem based learning (Sylvester et al., 2004; Grimes, 2015) dismantles the artificial subdivision of skills into separate compartments with defined boundaries. Recognizing the multidimensionality of the problems (Galowitz, 2012) stimulates the students to think in an interdisciplinary manner and favours an open approach to interdisciplinary cooperation among law students, students of other disciplines, and other professionals (Galowitz, 1999 & 2012).

Furthermore, teaching law through clinical legal education leads law professors to borrow methods and tools from fields of knowledge other than law, for example, the sciences of education, psychology and sociology. An obvious example of borrowing from the field of pedagogics is represented by the attention given by law lecturers to reflective learning and reflective practice (Schön, 1983).

The Legal Clinic as a Community of Practice

The paradigm shift applied by the legal clinics involves both the role of the teacher and the concept of the interpretation of law.

The bottom up process with which the clinics approach the learning of law is obviously the opposite to the current dogmatic approach of teaching law, which proceeds unidirectionally, in presuming that the professor has to and is able to transfer crystallized legal knowledge to the student. By immersing themselves in the contexts in which law in action takes shape, legal clinics come into contact with the social and professional groups operating within such contexts. This simultaneously achieves the loss of clear boundaries between who is teaching and who is learning, in other words the loss by the academic teacher of the monopoly of knowledge of the law.

In this respect, legal clinics may be looked on from the perspective of the community of practice, defined as "a group of people who share a concern, a set of problems, or a passion about a topic and who deepen their knowledge and expertise in this area by interacting on an ongoing basis" (Wenger, *et al*, 2002, p. 4).

Rather than referring to a social group dimension, this notion refers to the "social process of negotiating competence in a domain over time" (Farnsworth *et al.*, 2016, p. 143). The concept of the community of practice is theorised to underline that learning is a social process situated in a cultural and historical context. Learning in context takes places through people taking part in multiple social practices and that makes learning to be a socially constituted experience of meaning making. Moreover, this experience is placed "in the relation between the person and the social world as they constitute each other. The technical terms of the theory include negotiation of meaning, practice, community, identity and competence, among others" (ivi, p. 142).

As Wegner argues that knowing is an act of participation in "complex social learning systems" (2002, p. 226), the clinics are "places" where learning develops and knowledge becomes a means of constructing collectively, following the method of social constructivism.

As in the communities of practice, where there is no explicit hierarchy and roles are assumed on the basis of competence and the needs of the individuals, in the legal clinics the hierarchical relationship between teacher and student is reduced. Legal clinics within the continental European context show – perhaps more than in other settings –the typical character of the communities of practice: educators building "alliances with practitioner groups, licensing and accreditation bodies, and other key institutions of their field" (Ivi). In many European clinics, indeed, the learning process involves other figures of educators alongside the academic teacher, such as lawyers, and the learning in context almost always requires the active involvement of social players, such as NGOs, public authorities, professional operators and clients. The involvement of these latter players is very interesting because, even if these are mainly involved as recipients of the services offered by the legal clinics, they inevitably take on an active role in the community of practice, since the learning is precisely the product of the continuous mutual exchange of knowledge and experience that occurs locally between all the components of the community of practice.

It cannot be denied the close relationship between the legal clinics as communities of practice and the issue of power. Wenger argues that communities of practice "are always located in and shaped by broader fields in Bourdieu's sense". In the community of practice, however, "the field is not a given" since it is itself defined by the "negotiation of competence" that occurs within it (Farnsworth et al., 2016, p.151-152). The transformative power of knowledge that occurs within the community of practice is amplified by the fact that such communities are always located at the boundaries with other disciplines and other communities of professional practices and it is precisely at this boundary space that innovation often takes place (Ivi, p. 157).

The relationship between legal clinics and the interpretation of law fits in this context.

It has been observed that "one of the potentially transformative effects of communities of practice is to define, redefine and challenge our assumptions about legal education, and about lawyering itself" (Baron & Corbin, 2012, p.116). The realist approach to interpretation recognises that the rules do not possess a pre-constituted meaning completely independent of the processes in which and with which juridical operators employ those rules (Tarello, 1974, p. 393 -395). Moreover, the phenomenon of interpretation of law is not by any means the monopoly of judges and lawyers, but many other institutional and social players have a role in it, as well as lay people (Llewellyn 1930; Frank 1933; Kruse; 2011-2012).

Legal clinics, therefore, undeniably interpret the law. They act as original communities of interpretation (Viola & Zaccaria, 1999), as well as epistemic communities (Haas, 1992)[11]. By the reason of its nature, these are epistemic communities placed at the borders of the legal system, in many respects.

Far from the rigidity of academic roles, law professors, lawyers, NGO, social activists linked by the common aim to "transform legal education into justice education" (Bloch, 2013, p. 48) consider themselves as a part of the community of clinicians. This epistemic community may be considered as a phenomenon of transnationalism: the clinical movement today is taking shape and is developing through networks, which bring together meetings, workshops and training for trainers where legal clinicians meet to share competences, methodologies and experiences, both at international[12], regional[13] and local[14] levels. In this way the clinicians take part not only in the process of transnationalisation of educational practices, but also in the process of implementation of fundamental rights. The interpretation of the law, therefore, which is applied by the clinics, is certainly ideologically orientated by the principles and the values around which the clinical epistemic community recognises itself: the promotion of social justice, access to justice and observance of human rights. If clinicians, in relation to their view and description of law, may be placed on the constructivist horizon (Blengino, 2015, 2018b), the clinical epistemic community, on the proscriptive level, is strongly rooted to the aim of social justice and to substantial trust in the law (Barbera, 2018).

This is also the reason why the clinics today act in the *border* areas of law: the combination of empirical approach to law and social justice mission leads the clinics to intervene mainly in contexts where rights are denied, in grey or dark areas of law. In doing so, the clinics interpret the law, transforming it "by promoting an antiformalist method of interpreting law and hence of judicial application of the law" (Barbera, 2018, p.66) within its own "value" horizon.

---

11 The notion of epistemic community has been introduced by Haas (1992) referring to the context of international relationships. Over the years the concept has been deepened and extended to other areas. In a broad sense the epistemic community may be defined as a network of professionals, often from a variety of different disciplines, which produce policy-relevant knowledge about complex issues in their area of expertise (Haas, 1992, p. 16).

12 As Global Alliance for Justice Education (GAJE), //www.gaje.org.

13 In Europe, the European Network of Clinical Legal Education (ENCLE) was set up in 2012, www.encle.org.

14 For example, cf. Rete Italiana delle Cliniche Legali [Italian Network of the Legal Clinics] and Red española de Clínicas Jurídicas (http://clinicas-juridicas.blogspot.com/).

Reflective Practice in the Community of Practice

The community of the legal clinics considers "reflective practice as fundamental to effective lawyering and the professional identity formation of lawyers, including the pursuit of core values, social justice, and personal growth" (Balsam *et al.* 2017-18, p.46).

The introduction of reflective practice to continental European legal education is undoubtedly one of the more interesting fruits of the process of transnationalisation of didactic practices favoured by the exchanges within the movement of legal clinics.

The epistemology of practice theorised by Donald Schön (1983, p. 49) consider reflection in action and reflection on action as the professional nucleus of reflective practitioners, in other words, people who problematize action, reflect, analyse and give sense to their daily practice.

The reaction of Schön against an instrumental notion of teaching that considers a teacher as a technician evidently represents an important new idea in European legal education. Reflective practice fosters the idea that learning is a socially situated circular process and opposes the dogmatic approach of unidirectional law teaching.

Reflective practice is a collective process involving both teachers and students. It allows for the teachers to analyse students' observations, to identify and assess what they have learned, and to use the new knowledge in order to inform future actions. The development of this practice on the part of the teachers is therefore ordinarily connected with assessment of learning. At the same time, the students are placed at the center of the learning process, from where reflective practice allows them independently to reach a level of deep learning, resulting from the gained ability to develop a conceptual framework through experience and reflection on that experience (Piaget, 1950).

Learning does not end in knowledge and does not involve just rational aspects: "without reflection, clinical legal education" would become "simply skills acquisition or, at best, work-integrated learning" (Evans et *al* , 2017, p. 162).

In the learning process that is activated in the community of practice consisting of the legal clinic, reflective practice produces multiple benefits, because sharing skills and the learning of each of the participants – students, teachers and other players – can be better structured and organised.

Considering learning as "the process whereby knowledge is created through the transformation of experience" (Kolb, 1984, p. 38), the reflective diaries or the reflective cycles (Gibbs, 1988) help to make reflection *in* action – which risks to remain tacit, unconscious and unspoken – sufficiently problematized through a reflection *on action*, which is systematic and documented. The students learn from the teachers, from the social and institutional players they work with or from their peers and from the mental and emotional interaction with themselves, made possible by the tools of reflective practice. At the same time, the reflections and feedback from the students become valuable sources of learning, both for the educators and for the others involved in the clinic.

One of the most innovative aspects of reflective practice, which has not yet been sufficiently explored in the context of the European clinics, concerns the way in which this method allows people to approach not only education in itself, but also the juridical phenomenon (Blengino *et al.* 2019).

"Clinicians" observes Kruse "are naturally situated to answer the call for embedded research, which fits closely with the social justice goals and reflective practice methods…" (2011-12, p. 298).

In the legal clinics, students, and their teachers as well, are active participants in their own learning, which includes both discovering the gaps between law in the books and law in action and the identification of the best way to go about closing the distance. Reflective practice then also becomes a way of making reflection about action (Schulman, 1987).

Reflective practice therefore represents an extra, powerful "antidote to the technical/positivist nature of legal education" (Evans *et al*, 2017, p. 162) also because it is a perfect position from which to respond to the need for empirical research into law.

This is an opening towards the application of social research methods in the sphere of legal studies which is absolutely innovative in the tradition of continental legal education.

It has been observed that critical reflection is a research method (Fook, 2011). Reflective practice in the legal clinics therefore constitutes in itself a socio-legal epistemology of law.

The legal clinics represent a perfect tool for experimenting that "everyday problems are not simply pre-defined, but are constructed through our engagement with the 'intermediate zone of practice', which, typically, is characterized by uncertainty, uniqueness, and value conflict" (Schön, 1983, p. 6). As pointed out by Schön, in fact, true reflective practice comes not only from action or experience, but more specifically from the uncertainty, uniqueness and conflict of that experience. Through reflective practice students and teachers, by entering actively and systematically the process of problem based learning, become inquirers (Leicht & Day, 2000, p. 183) into their own practice and, therefore into the juridical problem they are dealing with.

The bottom up approach, through which the learning process prompted by the clinic is activated, leads the students to deal with real needs and multidimensional problems. By means of clinical experience, students observe law critically in context and through reflective practice they reflect on the ways in which the parties involved in legal procedures – including the clinic – act and interpret the law. In this way, the clinic identifies problems and questions and, subsequently, acts in the legal field to promote rights and access to justice in the most suitable way for the situation[15]

It is evident that this framework is the same as that on which action research is based (Lewin, 1946). This research methodology consists of analysis of a *practice* related to a field of social experience, with the aim of introducing into the *practice* itself some improving changes. This method is normally used by the practitioners themselves in the field of experience analysed and is widely used in the field of education, involving the educators as researchers.

How CLE Can Lead Students to Deeper Understand What Are Human Rights in Action

Action research and clinical legal education share a common goal. Both are oriented towards a concrete intervention and to achieve an improving change.

Holistic use of reflective practice and of action research (Leicht & Day, 2000) enables all the players of the clinical community of practice to achieve various advantages.

Some reflections on the potential and usefulness of the use of such an approach for the purposes of teaching, research and action may be formulated, using as an example the approach taken by the Human Trafficking

---

15   The various methods of organisation and intervention of the clinics, and their choice of intervention, with actions of legal aid, street law or community lawyering, are the consequence of empirical detection of the need for which the clinic is called on to answer. This way of conceiving the intervention of the clinic has led, for example, the legal clinic for detainees, run by the writer, to differentiate the activities of the students on the basis of the questions encountered: some recurring questions on the part of the detained persons have led to the publication of a comic guide explaining the rights and duties of the detainees (Blengino 2015; 2018a); the need to guarantee the right of the detainees with their minor children has led to an interdisciplinary intervention for architectural conversion of the spaces of the prison building (Blengino 2018b), and some cases of the prisoners' claims about the right to be forgotten have led the clinic to carry out activities more specifically of legal aid.

Clinic of the University of Turin in exploring and dealing with the phenomenon of trafficking.

Human trafficking for purposes of sexual exploitation is a phenomenon that is dramatically increasing in Europe and in Italy together with the migratory flows from the Sub-Saharan Africa. This is an issue that is currently of the utmost interest and not completely understood: the shortage of updated official data, the continual rapid changes of strategy by the traffickers and the psychological and cultural vulnerability of the victims make it very difficult to fully understand the dynamics of the phenomenon and to tackle it.

Over several years the Human Trafficking Clinic of the University of Turin has developed the multiple interest of actively intervening by offering legal support to the victims, attempting locally to achieve real understanding of the phenomenon and the procedures to contrast it, as well as proposing itself, on this basis, to help identify and share the best practices.

The peculiarities of the community of practice formed by this clinic can be traced back as far as its origins. As a concrete demonstration of the potential of the bottom up approach to teaching, the clinic was effectively planned and set up by a student group[16]: it was them who carried out a preliminary research into the field, to understand the local characteristics of the phenomenon and identify the needs and potential spaces for intervention for the clinic. They established a first contact with one of the most active anti-trafficking NGO in the local area and offered the expert juridical support for the girls seeking asylum who were housed in the structure because presumed victims of trafficking. Furthermore, the students involved the teachers, by asking us for availability to develop systematically a clinic on the issue of trafficking.

The clinic community of practice that was set up as a result of the student initiatives is today specifically structured and complex. It consists of professors , lawyers, students, intercultural mediators, experts on trafficking

---

16 The clinic arose originally from an idea of a group of students of the legal clinic for Prison and Rights at the University of Turin, who were called on to propose and experiment with a new clinic project by Prof. José García Añón of the University of Valencia, during a teaching stay in Turin (Blengino 2018a). Today, this clinic is fully operating under the direction of a team of teachers from the Department of Law of the University of Turin and from the International University College. The setting up and the first steps of this clinic project were presented by the promoting students and by the teachers involved in the presentation entitled "Law clinic in support of victims of human trafficking: experience from a student initiated activity in Piedmont/ Italy", which was presented at the 4th ENCLE meeting "Clinical Legal Education and Access to Justice for all: from asylum seekers to excluded communities", held in Valencia on 27 and 28 October 2016.

operating in the private social area and all the major NGOs engaged in identification of victims and combating trafficking in the region[17].

Together with the interdisciplinary équipe formed to create it, the project has progressively expanded and developed. Today this is structured
around the aim of lending legal support to the girls seeking asylum, mainly
Nigerians, for whom the local area commissions for recognition of international protection suspend their decision because they suspect that they are
in fact victims of trafficking. It becomes vital to carry out interviews with
these girls, for the purpose of verifying the existence of indicators making it
possible to identify them effectively as victims and give them the juridical
support they need to apply for protection as victims. This would recognise
them the right to stay officially in Italy, breaking the link of physical and
psychological subjection that binds them to their exploiters.

The complexity of the issue and the multiple interactions that are required
to provide this kind of legal support allowed us to appreciate the need to
organise the learning experience, so as to keep the unbreakable relationship
between reflection and transformative action (Beach, 2005) within the clinic.

This has meant, first of all, that the community of practice recognizes the
need to open up to synergic cooperation with the local institutions and the
NGOs already engaged in the area in combating human trafficking.

The fact that all the main associations engaged on the front of combating
trafficking in Piedmont are prepared to make use of the legal support of
the students represents an exceptional opportunity for the clinic to immerse
itself in the law in context.

After preliminary multidisciplinary training carried out jointly by teachers,
expert lawyers in the area of trafficking and operators from the local associations, the students of the legal clinic conduct interviews with the girls
seeking asylum. Collecting and reporting the girls' stories is done for the
purpose of identifying the existence of indications of trafficking and to prepare the girls for hearings with the local commissions. If appropriate, this
activity is followed up by drafting legal memories with the application to
the local commission for recognition of international protection; in other
circumstances the students lend juridical support to the associations through
drafting opinions.

The interviews are held on the premises of the associations, in the presence of the social operator and the cultural mediator from the association:
this means the students are working within the setting through which the
associations normally operate in real conditions.

The increased number of associations involved, and therefore the number
and variety of the interviews, has led us to question the way to face the risk

---

17 The clinic operates in Piedmont, an Italian north-western region.

that the increasing workload might reduce our attention to the process of individual learning for the students. At the same time we have realised our fortune in being offered the opportunity to operate on an extensive local area and thus be able to acquire through the legal clinic an overall picture of how the local system functions in combating trafficking.

It has also become progressively clear that the chance for the legal clinic to provide adequate juridical support to the victims of trafficking calls for identifying and setting up the various goals of learning in a precise manner. The students are required: to know the legislation and procedures for granting of international protection; to be aware of the processes and the role actually played by the institutional and social players in the various stages from identification to granting, or refusal, of international protection; to know how to prepare and conduct an interview with people who have language difficulties, cultural peculiarities and who find themselves in complicated emotive circumstances; to know how to identify during the interviews those juridical elements that help to identify the right to protection, to draft legal memories and prepare the girls for an interview before the local commission.

How, then, can we address the need to follow analytically the learning process of our students, immersed in complex situations and without our presence, without losing information that may be important both for the learning process and for understanding law in action?

Making use of the tool of the reflective cycle (Gibbs, 1988) and drafting reflective reports, after each interview on the part of the students is useful from various points of view.

It enables them not to lose information and to problematize their own action as well as those of the other players from the community of practice; it enables the teachers to supervise the activities of the students and, at the same time, re-plan, modify and improve the process of learning and action; and it enables both to acquire new skills based empirically on law in context.

For example, planning of the activities in accordance with the circular template *concrete experience – reflective observation – abstract conceptualisation – active experimentation* (Gibbs, 1988) enables the community of practice to understand how, even though the interview setting (consisting of the pair of students – operator – mediator and applicant) is identical in the various associations, different dynamics also come into play corresponding to the varying of the people. Such dynamics represent important extra-juridical variables that may condition in a significant manner the interview or the possibility of collecting all the required information and, consequently, the chance for the girls to be recognised as victims of human trafficking by the local commissions.

Reviewing on the experience and sharing between peers enables the students to reflect on their own actions and those of the others during the interviews and to acquire progressively the awareness needed for their own role in the setting of the interview. Without the aid of critical reflection it is easy for the students working together with the operators from the associations to succumb to the risk of assuming a subordinate role in relation to the practitioners. Operators and mediators are perceived as educators, because they are holders of knowledge and professional skill which the students do not have. Through reflective observation the students are able to critically observe their own actions as well as those of the others: it becomes clear to all that, in the community of practice, the roles blur and the various participants assume multiple roles, as educators and learners. Reflective observation is a key step for the students in acquiring awareness of the need for their active presence as legal experts in the interview and their usefulness for the work of the NGOs.

Collecting the stories of the girls represents a privileged observation point for appreciating the complexity of the phenomenon of trafficking on a local level and to acquire awareness of the continual challenges thrown down by the traffickers to concrete application of legislative instruments for safeguarding the victims of trafficking. From this point of view, the reflective diaries on the interviews and on the stories heard constitute invaluable metacognitive and research material.

Drafting the reflective practice reports after each interview makes it possible to realise the changes that occur during the progressive forming over time of the trust between the players in the interview setting or, on the other hand, the contradictions and reticence the girls sometimes display between one interview and the next. This makes it possible to identify punctually the factors that help or hinder the successful outcome of the interview and compromise effective access by the victims to the instruments of protection that the law formally recognises for them: the lack of understanding, on the part of the girls, of their own rights and instruments for their protection; the cultural and psychological barriers; fear of the effects of *voodoo* rites practised by their exploiters; concerns for family members left in their home country, or even the feeling of gratitude towards the exploiters who helped them get to Europe. These are elements that the lawyer must be aware of and that the students cannot get close to, unless through this type of experience.

The process of abstract conceptualisation, with which the students manage to operate the juridical 'encoding' of these elements, and identify the juridical solutions to the cases dealt with, is fundamental both for their education as reflective practitioners, and for the ability of the clinic to gain effectively access to justice for the victims.

The collective sharing of the reviewing on the experience enables, again, verification of how determined factors recur in the girls' stories and determines, in a definite manner, the possibility of an empirically based, systematic picture of the actual phenomenon. The usefulness of reflective practice as action research is also shown to the teachers, practitioners and operators of the NGOs: sharing points of view enables everyone to learn and re-think their own activities with a view to improvement. The difficulties the operators experience daily in their activities and their need to exchange and share skills, between peers and with the academic community of teachers and students, draw the benefit of support in the collective sharing of reviewing on the experience.

To sum up, the active experimentation that is a consequence of reflective practice in the community of practice may really be the fruit of a learning process and of shared critical reflection. This presumably will make the action more effective for all.

References

Amato, C. (2018). Experiential learning from the continental viewpoint: if the cap fits..., in R. Grimes (ed) *Re-thinking Legal Education under the Civil and Common Law. A Road Map for Constructive Change*, Routledge, London, p. 13 – 27.

Alaimo, C.M., Consigli, E., Romano, M. and A. Sciurba (2018). La clinica legale per i diritti umani dell'Università di Palermo, in A. Maestroni, P. Brambilla and M. Carrer (ed), *Teorie e pratiche nelle cliniche legali*, Giappichelli, Torino, p.161-189.

Asta, F., Caprioglio, C. and E. Rigo (2018). Il ruolo delle cliniche legali come strumento di insegnamento e approccio al diritto. L'esperienza della clinica del diritto dell'immigrazione e della cittadinanza di Roma III, in A. Maestroni, P. Brambilla and M. Carrer (ed), *Teorie e pratiche nelle cliniche legali,* Giappichelli, Torino, p.207-220.

Bailleux, A., François Ost (2013). "Droit, contexte et interdisciplinaritè: refondation d'une demarche", in *Revue interdisciplinaire d'études juridiques*, 1, 70, p. 25-44.

Balsam, J. S., S. L. Brooks, and M. Reuter (2017-2018). "Assessing Law

Students as Reflective Practitioners", in *N.Y. L. Sch. L. Rev.*, 62, 49, p. 45-67.

Barbera, M. (2018). The Emergence of an Italian Clinical Legal Education Movement: the University of Brescia Law Clinic, in A. Alemanno and L. Khadar (ed), *Reinventing Legal Education How Clinical Education is Reforming the Teaching and Practice of Law in Europe,* Cambridge University Press, p. 59-75.

Bartoli, C. (2015). "The Italian Legal Clinics Movement: Data and Prospects", in *International Journal of Clinical Legal Education.* 22, 2, p. 213-229.

Bartoli, C. (2016). "Legal clinics in Europe: for a commitment of higher education in social justice", in *Diritto & Questioni Pubbliche,* Special issue, May.

Beach, D. (2005). "The problem of how learning should be socially organized: relations between reflection and transformative action", in *Reflective Practice,* 6, 4, p. 473-489.

Blázquez-Martín, D. (2011). The Bologna Process and the Future of Clinical Education in Europe: A View from Spain", in F. Bloch (ed), *The Global Clinical Movement: Educating Lawyers for Social Justice,* Oxford University Press.

Blengino, C. (2015). Formare il giurista oltre il senso comune penale: il ruolo della clinical legal education in carcere, in C. Blengino (ed) *Stranieri e sicurezza. Il volto oscuro dello stato di diritto,* ESI, Napoli.

Blengino, C. (2018a). "Interdisciplinarity and Clinical Legal Education: how synergies can improve access to rights in prison", in *International Journal of Clinical Legal Education,* 25, 1, p. 210- 239.

Blengino, C. (2018b). Fondamenti teorici di una pratica: approccio bottom up, prospettiva interdisciplinare e impegno civile nella clinica legale con detenuti e vittime di tratta, in A. Maestroni, P. Brambilla and M. Carrer (ed), *Teorie e pratiche nelle cliniche legali,* Giappichelli, Torino, p. 233- 260.

Blengino C., Brooks S., Deramat M. and S. Mondino (2019), "Reflective Practice: Connecting Assessment and Socio-Legal Research in Clinical Legal Education", in *International Journal of Clinical Legal Education,* Special Issue, forthcoming.

Bloch, F. S. (2008), "Access to Justice and the Global Clinical Movement", in *Washington University Journal of Law & Policy,* p. 111 -139.

Bloch, F. S., ed. (2011). *The global clinical movement. Educating lawyers to social justice,* Oxford University Press.

Brooks, S.L. & Robert G. Madden (2011-2012). "Epistemology and Ethics in Relationship-Centered Legal Education and Practice", in *New York Law School Law Review,* 56, p. 331-366.

Cappelletti, M. (1979). Accesso alla giustizia: conclusione di un progetto internazionale di ricerca giuridico-sociologica, in *Foro Italiano,* 54, p.54-61.

Cappelletti, M. (ed) (1981). *Access to Justice and the Welfare State* vol. 4, European University Institute, Firenze, Lemonnier.

Carnelutti, F. (1935). "Le cliniche del diritto". *Rivista di diritto Procedurale Civile,* 2, 1, p. 169-175.

Charmaz, K. And A. Bryant, (2007. *The Sage book of Grounded Theory,* Sage, London.

De Sousa Santos, B. (2012). La Universidad en el siglo XXI. Para una reforma democratica y emancipadora de la Universidad, in R. Ramirez (ed) *Tranformar la universidad para transformar la sociedad,* 2nd ed. Quito, Senescyt, p. 139-194.

De Sousa Santos, B. (2016). *The Universities at a Crossroads,* in Grosfoguel R., Hernandez, R. and Velasquez, R.R. *Decolonizing the Westernized University,* Lanham Maryland, Lexington Books, p. 295-302.

Evans A., Cody A., Copeland A., Giddings J., Joy P., Noone M. A., and S. Rice, (2017). Reflective practice: The essence of clinical legal education in *Australian Clinical Legal Education: Designing and Operating a Best Practice Clinical Program in an Australian Law School,* p. 153-178.

Farnsworth, V., Kleanthous, I., and E. Wenger-Trayner, (2016). "Communities of Practice as a Social Theory of Learning: A Conversation with Etienne Wenger", in *British Journal of Educational Studies,* 64, 2, p. 139-160.

Fernández-Artiach, P., García-Añón J. and R. Mestre i Mestre (2017). Birth, growth and reproduction of Clinical Legal Education in Spain, in Richard Grimes (ed.), *Re-imagining legal education under the civil and common law.* Routledge, London, p. 145-154.

Fook, J. (2011). Developing critical reflection as a research method, in J. Higgs, A. Tichen A, Horsfall D. and D. Bridges (ed), *Creative Spaces for Qualitative Researching,* Sense Publishers, Rotterdam, p.55-64.

Galowitz, P. (1999). "Collaboration Between Lawyers and Social Workers: Re-examining the Nature and Potential of the Relationship", in *Fordham L. Rev.* 2123, 67.

Galowitz, P. (2012). "The opportunities and challenges of an interdisciplinary clinic", in *International Journal of Clinical Legal Education,* 18, p.165 – 180.

García-Añón, J. (2013). Transformation in Legal Teaching and Learning: Clinical Legal Education as a Transformative Component, in J. García-Añón (Ed.) *Transformaciones en la Docencia y Enseñanza del Derecho. Actas del V Congreso Nacional de Docencia en Ciencias Jurídicas* Unitat d'Innovació Educativa – University of Valencia.

García-Añón, J. (2014), "La integración de la educación jurídica clínica en el proceso formativo de los juristas" in *REDU*, 12, 3, p.153-175.

García-Añón, J. (2017). Teaching and learning legal ethics and professional responsibility under the civil law, in Richard Grimes (Ed.), *Re-thinking legal education under the civil and common law.* Routledge: London, p. 96- 103.

Gascón-Cuenca, A. (2016). "The Evolution of the Legal Clinical Methodology at the Spanish Universities: opportunities and challenges posed by the Strategic Litigation at the Human Rights Clinic", in *Revista de Educación y Derecho. Education and Law Review* 14, p. 1-15.

Glaser B. G. and A. Strauss (1967). *The Discovery of Grounded Theory*, Aldine de Gruyter, New York.

Gibbs, G. (1988). *Learning by doing: A guide to Teaching and Learning Methods*, FEU, Birmingham.

Grimes, R. (2015). "Problem-based learning and legal education – a case study in integrated experiential study", in *REDU*, 13, 1, p. 361-375.

Khun, T. (1970 2nd edition), *The Structure of Scientific Revolutions,* University of Chicago Press, Chicago.

Kennedy, D. (2004). *Legal Education and the Reproduction of Hierarchy A Polemic Against the System*, New York University Press, New York.

Kolb, D. A. (1984). *Experiential Learning: Experience as the Source of Learning and Development.* Englewood Cliffs, Prentice Hall, New York.

Kruse, K. (2011). "Getting Real About Legal Realism, New Legal Realism and Clinical Legal Education", in *New York Law School Law Review*, 56, p. 659-684.

Haas, P. (1992). "Introduction: Epistemic communities and international policy coordination" , in *International Organization,* 46, 1, p. 1-35.

Leitch, R. and C. Day (2000). "Action research and reflective practice: towards a holistic view", in *Educational Action Research*, 8, 1, p. 79-193.

Lewin, K. (1946). "Action Research and Minority Problems", in *Journal of Social Issues*, 2, p. 34-46.

Llewellyn, K. (1935). "On What is Wrong with So-Called Legal Education", in *Columbia Law Review*, 35, p. 651-678.

Maestroni, A., Brambilla, P. and Carrer, M. (ed.), (2018), *Cliniche Legali in Italia Vol. II Cliniche Legali tra teorie e pratiche,* Torino. Giappichelli.

Marella, M.R. and Rigo, E. (2015). "Cliniche legali, Commons e giustizia sociale". In *Parolechiave,* 1, p.181-194.

Perelman, J. (2014). "Penser la pratique, théoriser le droit en action: des cliniques juridiques et des nouvelles frontières épistémologiques du droit", in *Revue interdisciplinaire d'études juridiques* 72, 2, p. 133-153.

Piaget, J. (1950). *The Psychology of Intelligence.* Routledge, London.

Poillot, E. (2014). *L'enseignement clinique du droit. Expériences croisées et perspective pratique,* Larcier, Brussels.

Poillot, E. (2016). Comparing Legal Clinics: is there a way to a European Clinical Culture? The Luxemburg Experience, in A. Abbignente (ed.) *La diffusione dell'insegnamento clinico in Italia e in Europa: radici teoriche e dimensioni pratiche,* ESI, Napoli.

Schön, D. (1983). *The Reflective Practitioner: How Professionals Think In Action,* Basic Books, New York.

Schulman L. (1987). "Knowledge and Teaching. Foundations of the New Reform", in *Harvard Educational Review,* 1, 57, p. 1-21.

Sylvester C. J. Hall, E. Hall, (2004). "Problem – based learning and clinical legal education: what can clinical educators learn from PBL?" in *International Journal of Clinical Legal Education,* 4, p. 39-64.

Tarello, G. (1974), *Diritto, enunciati, usi,* Il Mulino, Bologna.

Tokarz, K. (2006). *"Poverty, Justice, and Community Lawyering: Interdisciplinary and Clinical Perspectives",* in *Washington University Journal of Law and Policy,* 20, p. 101-168.

Tomeo, V. (2013). *Il diritto come struttura del conflitto. Un'analisi sociologica,* Rubbettino.

Viola, F. and G. Zaccaria (1999). *Diritto e interpretazione. Lineamenti di teoria ermeneutica del diritto,* Laterza, Roma-Bari.

Vogliotti, M. (2014). La fine del grande stile, in V. Barsotti (ed), *L'identità delle scienze giuridiche in ordinamenti multilivello. Quaderni del dottorato fiorentino in scienze giuridiche,* Maggioli, Firenze.

Vogliotti, M. (2018) (ed), *Pour une nouvelle éducation juridique,* L'Harmattan, Paris.

Wegner, E., R. McDermott and W. M. Snyder (2002). *Cultivating Communities of Practice: A Guide to Managing Knowledge,* Harvard Business Review.

Wilson, R. (2009). *Western Europe: Last Holdout in the Worldwide*

Acceptance of Clinical Legal Education, German Law Journal 10, 7, p. 823-846.

Wilson, R. (2011). Beyond legal imperialism. US Clinical Legal Education and the New Law and Development, in F. Bloch (ed). *The global clinical movement. Educating lawyers to social justice*, Oxford. Oxford University Press, p. 135-150.

Wenger-Trayner, E., Fenton-O'Creevy M., Hutchinson, S., Kubiak, C., and B. Wenger-Trayner (2014). *Learning in landscapes of practice. Boundaries, identity, and knowledgeability in practice-based learning*, Routledge, Abingdon.

Wilson, R. (2017) (ed). *The Global Evolution of Clinical Legal Education. More than a Method*. Cambridge University Press.

Andrés Gascón-Cuenca[1]

The Crisis of the Welfare State and the Worsening of Access to Justice: The Role of the University and of the Clinical Legal Movement in Spain and Italy

Not only Spain and Italy share a history of cultural exchange that has influenced our legal systems, but also we developed a particular Welfare State model, the Mediterranean one, that has a number of specific characteristics that distinguish it from other European models (Esping-Andersen, 2000; Moreno, 2001). Recently, both States were heavily hit by the economic crisis that began in 2008, which started to make its greatest impact as from 2010 and involved large budget cuts. Departing from this reality, this article researches into how the management of the crisis done by the Spanish and the Italian governments led to a dramatic reduction in the fundamental rights guaranteed for citizens, with an specific reference to access to justice, and of how vis-à-vis this reality, the legal clinical movement started to rise and spread in both national territories with the aim of meeting the needs of citizens at the new boundaries of the law.

The Crisis of the Mediterranean Welfare State Model: Distinctive Characteristics of Spain and Italy.

Starting from the theorizing about welfare states carried out by Espin-Andersen (1993), and the subsequent development of the Southern European Welfare model, or the Mediterranean one which Ferrera (1995), Abrahamson

---

1 Human Rights Institute. University of Valencia (Spain). Postdoctoral researcher. Generalitat Valenciana APOSTD/2017/093. Member of the research project: Transformaciones de la justicia. Autonomía, inequidad y ejercicio de derechos (DER2016-78356-P).

(1995), as well as Moreno (2001) have theorized, Spain and Italy not only share a similar history and culture influenced by their geographic position, but both States also partake a welfare state system with distinctive characteristics that distinguish them from other European countries such as France or Germany. This is characterized by low public spending or by the crucial role of family networks in service provision. The significant dualization (Ferrera, 1995) of the Italian and Spanish societies is particularly noteworthy as regards labor rights. On the one hand, we can identify those workers who have a regular link with the labor market and who will gain a high level of protection from the system; and on the other hand, workers who have an irregular relation with this market, that will be penalized with lower benefits and a worse access to and guarantee of certain rights.

Certainly, there are differences to be considered between these countries when we refer to the macroeconomic structure, that have to be pointed out even briefly in this section. Italy reached a democratic regime 30 years before Spain did, being a founding Member State of the European Union. Moreover, it has a developed industrial sector which has also preceded the Spanish one by many years, thereby being able to build strong commercial ties with the majority of the powerful European countries, resulting in the Italian GDP being always higher than the Spanish one (EUROSTAT, 2017).[2]

Considering these differences, it is also certain that the economy of both States was strongly affected by the crisis of the financial market which began in the United States of America in 2008, and which had a particular impact on these countries starting from 2010 on. Following economic directives of both the International Monetary Fund and the European Union, significant restrictions were imposed on public spending that entailed a significant reduction in the expenditure allocated to the welfare state. A pressure that was exerted with the objective that both States adapted their social protection systems "to the European logic of neoliberal globalisation" (Rodríguez Cabrero, 2016. See also: Guillén et. al., 2016). This action had a special impact on key areas for society like health, education, family support policies, or access to justice, that had their greatest impact amongst the young, women, and the immigrant population. This circumstance places them as groups in a situation of vulnerability due to the important limitations on fundamental rights that the application of these expenditure reduction policies implied.

The management of the distinctive features of the crisis implied the conversion of a significant amount of private debt into public debt, socializing its payment, to be covered by the funds that were being allocated to finance the Welfare State, via economic systems reforms (Ridaura Martínez, 2012).

---

2 Data available at: http://ec.europa.eu/eurostat/statistics-explained/index.php?title=File:GDP_at_current_market_prices,_2006_and_2014-2016_YB17.png

This situation resulted in very harsh social expenditure and labor market adjustments that have affected basic principles of these States, such as solidarity and the general access to the rights guaranteed by the Constitutions through the establishment and development of the welfare system (Rodríguez Cabrero, 2016; Guillén et. al., 2016). A situation that forced Italy and Spain to introduce drastic measures within its rights acknowledgement classifications, that led to the de-universalization of some (such as health), and the privatization of others, relying once again on the family as an instrument on which to resort to for the people that were excluded from the system due to these cuts (Hemerijck, 2013). Reforms that had as their objective the reduction of the purchasing power of wages and of social and labor rights, together with the weakening of public services and the *rationalization* of social protection (Guillén et. al., 2016).

A direct result of these *austerity* policies is the increase in the social risks connected with poverty or social exclusion, inequality, and the long-term unemployed. The 2016 at-risk-of poverty or social exclusion rate (EUROSTAT, 2016)[3] shows that during the period 2015-2016 in Italy the number of people at risk thereof increased up to 30% of the population, while in Spain slightly decreased to 27.9%. In both cases the figures show dramatic situations that affect a third of the total populatio

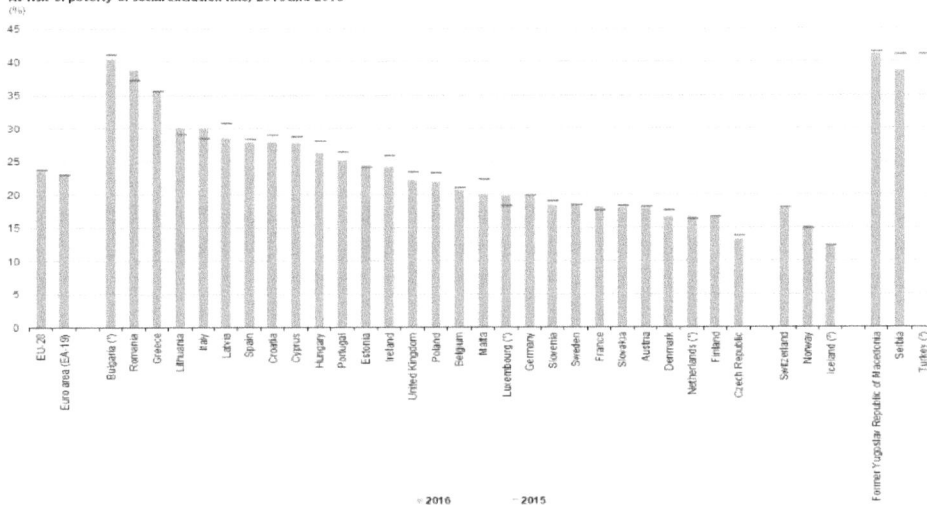

At-risk-of poverty or social exclusion rate, 2015 and 2016

(¹) Break in series.
(²) 2016: provisional.
(³) 2016: not available.
Source: Eurostat (online data code: ilc_peps01)

eurostat

---

3 http://ec.europa.eu/eurostat/statistics-explained/index.php?title=People_at_risk
_of_poverty_or_social_exclusion.

The same applies when we observe the figures of long-term unemployment. Once again, according to EUROSTAT (2018)[4] data, in 2017 people that have not found work during 12 months or more, amongst the whole unemployed people, were a total of 49% in the case of Italy and 35% in the case of Spain. Almost 5 unemployed Italians out of 10 and 4 unemployed Spanish out of 10 have not found a job for 12 months or more. This has as a direct consequence that the Gini index[5], that measures the extent to which the distribution of income within a country deviates from a perfectly equal distribution, shows an inequality for 2016 with a deviation of 34.5 in the Spanish case while it is 31.1 in Italy.

In general, this deterioration of the economic scenario, of access to employment and of social protection has led, as argued, to the increase in inequality and to the exclusion of large sectors of the population that have witnessed how welfare protection that were previously guaranteed cease to be so. This circumstance worsened their overall situation, inciting the struggle for scarce resources between the members of society.

Access to Justice in a Time of Economic Crisis

Once the main consequences of the austerity policies and their impact on society are generally introduced, this section aims to concretely analyze the consequences that expenditure cuts have had on access to justice, at a time when we have observed in the Spanish and Italian context[6], a development of policies of criminalization of behaviors that were not classified as such until then, or the increase in fines for petty offences or misdemeanors. Thus, this section will be structured in two areas: firstly, an analysis will be made of the meaning of access to justice from a substantive and formal point of view; and secondly, it will be critically observed how the legal changes introduced during the economic crisis put at risk guaranteed international standards of protection of human rights, particularly at a time during which it that has become clear that the expansion of sanctioning regulations (both penal and administrative) is an obvious trend within our legal systems.

---

4 Data available at: http://appsso.eurostat.ec.europa.eu/nui/submitViewTableAction.do

5 A coefficient of 0 expresses perfect equality where everyone has the same income, while a coefficient of 100 expresses full inequality where only one person has all the income.

6 It is sufficient to think here, for example, about the amendment to the Organic Law 4/2015, of 30th of March, of Protection of the Security of Spanish citizens (Official State Bulletin no. 77, 31st of March 2015), or the introduction of the Italian Minniti decree (Official Bulletin, general series, no. 40 of 17th February 2017).

Defining the Right of Access to Justice

It is not an easy task to define the topic of the right of access to justice. Moreover, this article does not expect to carry out its detailed analysis since it is beyond its objective and it is a work that has already been completed extensively and recently by other authors (Añón Roig, 2018; García Añón, 2018; Juan-Sanchéz, 2018). The task done in this piece of research is to identify the main international protection standards set by the existing international legislation in Italy and in Spain, in order to be able to critically analyze the legal reforms passed in these legal systems.

In this regard, the difficulty of defining both the substantial and the formal aspects of access to justice lies, as García Añón (2016, 2018) and Añón Roig (2013, 2016, 2018) point out, in its consideration as a multidimensional right that does not only include the right to have rights, but also its actual recognition and the need of its protection from the formal and the substantial point of view. Thus, United Nations (UN) defines the right to access to justice as a basic principle of the rule of law. In its absence, people are unable to have their voice heard, exercise their rights, challenge discrimination or hold decision-makers accountable for their decisions. The UN has been actively working in the area of access to justice. As a consequence, the declaration of the High-level Meeting on the Rule of Law of 2012, emphasizes in its paras. 14 and 15, the right of equal access to justice for all, including members of vulnerable groups, reaffirming the commitment of Member States to taking all necessary steps to provide fair, transparent, effective, non-discriminatory and accountable services that promote access to justice for all. From this statement one can begin to observe how the right of access to justice is essential in any democratic rule of law State, since it is connected with the recognition of rights and its substantial safeguard, and hence its multidimensionality.

Accordingly, starting by analyzing its formal or procedural aspects, we have to refer to the international agreements and covenants that regulate access to justice. This is not an easy task since it is a right that is recognized in a large number of treaties in very different ways. Thus, at United Nations level, article 14 of the International Covenant of Civil and Political Rights (ICCPR) states: "The right to equality before the courts and tribunals and to a fair trial is a key element of human rights protection and serves as a procedural means to safeguard the rule of law. Article 14 of the Covenant aims at ensuring the proper administration of justice, and to this end guarantees a series of specific rights"[7]. Here we can observe the multidimensionality referred to by García Añón (2016, 2018) and Añón Roig (2013, 2016, 2018). The nature of Article

---

7 General Comment No. 32. Right to Equality Before Courts and Tribunals and to a Fair Trial, CCPR/C/GC/32, 2007, para 2.

14 ICCPR is a complex one, as it combines different proceeding guarantees and scopes of application. The most relevant ones are, firstly, the guarantee of equality before the courts applicable regardless of the nature of the proceedings, and secondly, the granting to individuals of a fair and public hearing by a competent, independent and impartial tribunal established by law.

Moreover, the General Comment No. 32 of the Human Rights Committee, specially focused on the interpretation of Article 14 ICCPR, states that: "the access to the administration of justice must effectively be guaranteed in all cases to ensure that no individual is deprived, in procedural terms, of his/her right to claim justice. The right of access to courts and tribunals and equality before them is not limited to citizens of States parties, but must also be available to all individuals"[8]. Moreover, it continues assuring the importance of guaranteeing legal aid. Even though Article 14 of the ICCPR only recognizes the right to legal aid in criminal proceedings, the General Comment strongly "encourages States to provide free legal aid in other cases, for individuals who do not have sufficient means to pay for it" [9].

Focusing on the European level, articles 6 and 13 of the European Convention on Human Rights (ECHR) and articles 47 and 48 of the Charter of Fundamental Rights of the European Union (CFREU), set a series of standards to be observed by Member States. Although there are important differences between the two legal texts, as the ECHR grants the following rights under criminal charges, and the CFREU extends them to all the procedures that can be followed under the EU legislation, both bodies protect similar rights. They are the right to: a fair trial, receive information about the cause of accusation, legal aid, access to an effective remedy, be advised and presumption of innocence.

Thus, the analysis of the international standards mentioned above reveals an expansion in the scope of the right to access to justice, making several connections between the latter and other public interests and objectives to be protected by a democratic rule of law State (Añón Roig, 2018). If we examine the European Court of Human Rights (ECtHR) case law, we can perceive this reality. In the case of *Airey v. Ireland*, the ECtHR has decided that even though article 6 of the ECHR does not establish legal aid in civil cases, States are compelled to provide it when legal aid is indispensable for securing effective access to a court (FRA, 2016). This statement underlines the importance of access to adequate legal representation before the courts, not only in criminal cases, but also in other matters that might be complex or require the participation of experts.

Nevertheless, one important point that is not addressed by the ECHR, ECtHR or the CFREU is the means and merit tests that individuals have to

---

8 Ibid., para 9.

9 Ibid., para 10.

comply with in order to be eligible for free legal aid. In the case of *Steel and Morris v. the United Kingdom*, the ECtHR affirmed that "it is not incumbent on the State to seek through the use of public funds to ensure total equality of arms between the assisted person and the opposing party, as long as each side is afforded a reasonable opportunity to present his or her case under conditions that do not place him or her at a substantial disadvantage vis-à-vis the adversary"[10]. So States can freely determine the standards that individuals must reach in order to access the free of charge legal representation provided by them (FRA, 2016). As I will point out in the subsequent paragraphs, this is an important shortcoming in the protection of the right to access to justice. During times of economic recession, Italy and Spain enacted laws that raised these means and merit tests without further justification curtailing the access to justice to a great number of people, leaving them aside.

Furthermore, regarding the substantial content of the right to access to justice, it includes a "heterogeneous range of possibilities recognized by the legal systems concerning the knowledge of the access channels, means of appeal and the formal and informal conflict management services" (Añón Roig, 2018). As argued by Cromwell (2012), the right to access to justice has to meet a set of criteria that allow individuals to effectively access to the justice system and obtain an adequate answer to their requests. If not, procedural means to guarantee the access to justice are paper tiger.

Thus, the Convention on the Elimination of All Forms of Discrimination Against Women incorporates from the substantial point of view six interrelated, universal and immediately applicable components that are necessary to ensure access to justice for victims. They are: justiciability, availability, accessibility, good quality, provision of remedies for victims and accountability of justice systems[11].

Moreover, the United Nations Principles and Guidelines on Access to Legal Aid in Criminal Justice Systems published in 2013, contain an Annex that incorporates a list of principles and guidelines that should be observed by Member States. They are based on the recognition that States should undertake a series of measures, for them to maximize the positive impact that the establishment and reinforcement of a properly working legal aid system may have on an appropriately functioning criminal justice system and on access to justice (UN, 2013). It specifically refers in its *Guideline 12* to the funding of a nationwide legal aid system, encouraging States to support university law clinics. Even though, as above-mentioned, we have

---

10 ECtHR, case of Steel and Morris v. the United Kingdom, para. 62.

11 Committee on the Elimination of Discrimination Against Women. General Recommendation No. 33 on women's Access to justice, 2015. https://tbinternet.ohchr.org/_layouts/treatybodyexternal/Download.aspx?symbolno=CEDAW/C/GC/33&Lang=en

to recall that at UN level the international covenants and documents only recognize the access to financial benefits and cost savings of legal aid services throughout the criminal justice process, it is paramount to underline that in these Principles and Guidelines the UN calls out for the identification of fiscal mechanisms for channeling funds to legal aid. *Guideline 12* asks for "allocating a percentage of the State's criminal justice budget to legal aid services that are commensurate with the needs of effective legal aid provision", and "using funds recovered from criminal activities through seizures or fines to cover legal aid for victims" (UN, 2013). Moreover, it acknowledges that the budget for legal aid should cover a full range of services besides representation in court. Adequate special funding should be dedicated to defense expenses such as: costs for copying relevant files, documents and collection of evidence, expenses related to expert witnesses and forensics, social workers, and journey costs; and payments should be done timely.

From all the above-mentioned, we can conclude that the right to access to justice, within the context of the social and democratic rule of law State, develops a broad and crucial role in the Welfare State protection model (Añon Roig, 2018). On the one hand, it is necessary to guarantee the access to the legal system on equal terms (formal equality), but on the other hand, it is basic in advanced societies that base many of its social relations on conflict among their citizens, the provision of substantial contents to the rights they have been entitled to (substantial equality). Accordingly, Cappelletti & Garth (1979) exposed this dilemma many decades ago. They argued that in a laissez-faire system, legal poverty (the impossibility of people to have full access to the law and its institutions) is not an issue to be addressed by the State, "justice, like other commodities in the system, could be purchased only by those who could afford its costs, and those who could not were considered the only ones responsible for their fate" (Cappelletti & Garth 1979). So, there was only a formal, and not substantial, access to justice.

Nevertheless, in our time and how we have come to see, the recognition of access to justice as a human right is safeguarded both nationally and internationally (Francioni, 2007). Our national legal systems have as essential bases Constitutions that guarantee the protection of a number of fundamental rights, amongst which we find access to justice. Its protection is vital, firstly, as a support that enables to exercise other fundamental rights that may be affected by the conflictual relations that were previously mentioned, and secondly, as an empowerment tool (Van de Meene & Van Rooji, 2008), of all the people who make up society, who may go to court on equal terms to demand the protection of their rights (Anderson & Honneth, 2004).

Although formal access to justice has been widely accepted as a basic social right in our societies (Cappelletti & Garth, 1979; Añón Roig, 2018), substantive access to justice is more debated. As suggested by Cappelletti & Garth (1979) «optimal effectiveness in the context of a given substantive law could be expressed as complete "equality of arms"- the assurance that the ultimate result depends only on the relative legal merits». Even though they recognize that perfect equality is an idealistic concept, it is crucial to identify the obstacles that might jeopardize it. Both Cappelletti & Garth (1979) and Francioni (2007), specifically identify the cost of litigation as a barrier that might exclude sectors of the population from going to court. This is the area that will be developed in the following section.

Cost of Litigation, Access to Legal Aid Services and the Boundaries of the Legal Systems

In this section, as anticipated and once the study of the contents of the right of access to justice has been carried out, we will research into the Legal Aid Services' economic thresholds, introduced in the Spanish and the Italian legal systems, in order to critically analyze if they are an obstacle that might endanger the guarantee of the right to access to justice.

Identifying access to justice as a social right implies that it requires affirmative actions from the State towards its fulfilment. As stated by Añón Roig (2018), "the paradigm of Social Rights implies substantive modifications in the conception of the guarantees of rights, as it understands the recognition of vital rights as a condition for the exercise of other fundamental ones". Consequently, the State has a prominent role in ensuring, protecting and attaining access to justice for all the population, independently of their economic status, as it recognizes "conflict as a part of the core of social relations and the Law as an instrument for redistribution and commodification" (Añón Roig, 2018). In this light, now is the time to analyze the thresholds imposed by Spanish and the Italian legislations to have access to free legal advice. As identified by Cappelletti & Garth (1979), the cost of litigation is quite expensive in modern societies. Not only attorney fees are important, but also the liability of a losing party to bear the costs of the winning one is a deterrent for people to go to court.

Firstly, starting with the Spanish regulation, Article 119 of the Spanish Constitution recognizes that access to the legal system must be free for those who do not have enough resources to litigate. Thus, article 3 of *Law 1/1996, of 10th of January on Free Legal Aid*, develops this constitutional right and establishes the boundaries to its recognition, identifying the following thresholds: twice the IPREM (Spanish Public Income Indicator Multiplier) for people living on their own (gross monthly income of 1,075.68€); two and a half times the IPREM for people living in households with three people or less (gross monthly income of 1,344.60€, summing up the gross monthly income of all household members); three times the IPREM for households of four or more people (gross monthly income of 1,613.52€, adding up the gross monthly income of all household members).

Thus, these numbers show and set a clear boundary in access to justice. A family of three, formed by a single parent and two minors that earns 1,344.60 euros per month, is out of the system. A family formed by two parents and two children, in which only one of the parents work, earning 1,613.52 euros, is also out of the system. In a society that has reached unemployment rates of 26.3% in 2013, 20.5% in 2016 and 16.1% in February 2018, examples like there are sadly common. These families have to give it a second thought before starting any kind of court procedure for claiming their rights. It is impossible to add, on top of all the expenses a family has, not only lawyer fees but also the possibility of losing the case and the obligation to pay the winning party's costs.

Moreover, in 2012 the Spanish legislator passed the Law 10/2012, of 20th of November, named *Ley por la que se regulan determinadas tasas en el ámbito de la Administración de Justicia y del Instituto Nacional de Toxicología y Ciencias Forenses*, an Act that imposed fees for a long list of judicial proceedings, in particular cassation appeals and nullity actions. Even though in 2015[12] the Government revoked the fees for individuals, they were in force for more than two years, the most complicated period of the economic crisis. In 2016, the Constitutional Court[13] also declared unconstitutional some fees from legal entities. This Act was a serious pitfall (del Carpio Fiestas, 2012; Ruiz Garijo, 2013) for all individuals that tried to claim their rights, essentially because it did not establish a proportional system when stating the amounts of the fees to be paid by individuals (Martínez Sánchez, 2013). For instance, at the time it was in force, individuals that were struggling with their mortgages that sued their banks for evicting[14] them from their homes (Mestre-i-Mestre, 2018) had to face high fees for this legal proceeding, that frequently ended up increasing their debt with the bank. An eviction system that, incidentally, was outlawed by the European Court of Justice in 2013[15], as it was abusive towards consumers and did not

---

12   Revoked by Royal Decree-Law 1/2015, of 27th February,on the second opportunity mechanism,, reduction of the fiscal burden and other social measures.

13   Judgement of the Spanish Constitutional Court No. 140/2016, July 21, 2016.

14   During the economic crisis, the people evicted from their homes increased dramatically. In 2012, 46,408 families lost their home, 39,206 in 2013, and 45,298 in 2014. Consejo General del Poder Judicial, *Justicia dato a dato* Issues of 2012, 2013 and 2014.

15   Sentence of the European Court of Justice (first chamber), March 14, 2013. Case of

respect the rights protected by EU legislation.

Secondly, when it comes to the Italian free legal advice service, the situation is no better. The Italian regulations[16] set a threshold of 11,493.82 € per household without further proportionality (Trapella, 2013). That means that a family of 4 with just one of their members working and earning 12,000€ per year is out the system. These regulations establish a very low income that clearly sets a boundary in access to justice. It, not only does not consider the real cost of accessing the legal system, but also ignores the expenses that extrajudicial advice generates (Santoro, 2014). Moreover, as Ferraris argues, even though free legal advice is a matter of constitutional importance (like in the Spanish context), "the issue emerges when one is confronted with current events that get media attention and has a tendency to change into a discussion on whether free aid is worthy or not" (Ferraris, 2014).

As we have seen, although litigation costs were identified by Cappelletti & Garth (1979) many years ago as being one of the very first barriers for people to fight for their rights in court, the Italian and the Spanish legal systems have very low economic thresholds that limit access to free legal advice services for people in the lower income brackets. Thus, this limitation has been enforced in a time when social conflict levels are increasing. As above-mentioned, in 2015 Spain changed the Protection of Public Safety Act. This new regulation affects the guarantees of many fundamental rights (Bilbao Ubillos, 2015), but it has been used in particular by the Government to empty the constitutional freedom to peaceful public assembly by punishing political dissent with a wide range of administrative fines used towards people demonstrating against the cuts in the public budget (Bondia García, 2018). Such limitations fall short of respecting the international standards identified in the previous sections, as they do not guarantee the equality of arms protected by the ECtHR. With such low means and merit tests, the chances for individuals in the lower income brackets to have an opportunity to present their cases under conditions that do not place them in a substantial disadvantage versus the adversary are very reduced, as judicial and extrajudicial costs are considerable in our societies.

In this scenario, where certain boundaries to the law have been drawn, it is time to analyze the role that public universities, legal clinics and law

---

Mohamed Aziz v. Caixa d'Estalvis de Catalunya, Tarragona i Manresa (Catalunyacaixa).

16   L. 25/2005 – Modifications to the unique text on the legislative and regulatory provisions on the subject of legal charges, whereof the President of the Republic's decree 30th May 2002, no. 115; L. 134/2001 – Amendments to the law 30th July 1990, no. 217, setting out the establishment of legal aid financed by the State for the least well-off; and DPR 115/2002 – Unique text on the legislative and regulatory provisions on the subject of legal charges.

students have in the protection of fundamental rights.

The Role of Universities, Legal Clinics and Law Students in the Protection of Human Rights

In accordance with the opinion of Sousa Santos (2016), universities are presently at a crossroads. In order to decide which direction to choose, we have to carry out an important task of reviewing where we come from and where we would like to go. The well-known Bologna Process that started almost 10 years ago set the basis for a change, that at least initially was thought to be a step forward in the quality of public university curricula and education. Nevertheless, deeper fluctuations between positive and negative situations have occurred since the creation of the European Higher Education Area (EHEA) in 1999 that have directly affected its development. Thus, in this section, I will firstly analyze the role public universities should have in the promotion of social justice and of human rights values in general, and secondly, the active role that legal clinics must play, on the one hand, in training lawyers that have a critical vision of the legal order as a system that tends to reproduce hierarchy and power structures linked to discrimination patterns, and on the other hand, in recognizing the social needs of the people who have been left aside by the welfare state, as we have seen in the previous sections, and cannot fight for their rights in equality of arms.

Thus, since the founding of the EHEA the university, not only as an education institution but also as a social actor, is going through a steady period of paradigm shift. This is occurring in a time when the word *crisis* is playing a paramount role on paper: financial crisis, migration crisis, European model crisis, and so forth. As Sousa Santos (2016) says, "the university is being confronted with strong questions for which it has so far provided only weak answers". These strong questions formulated by him unveil the major challenges that universities, not only in the European context, but globally, are facing. Here I will only examine a couple of them very related to each other, because a deeper analysis of all of them exceeds the scope of this section.

The first important area to investigate is how to overcome the past 30 years' tendency to transform "the truth value of knowledge into the «market truth» value of knowledge" (Sousa Santos, 2016). This change has put on the ropes the efforts made by faculty members who are critical and nonconformist with this process of changing the values of university education, and who stand for training students that are competent critics of the legal system (Lloredo Alix, 2019). This means recognizing the role that the university has in civil society in order to challenge and dismantle the neoliberal unidirectional messages with which the market floods society, promoting legal ethics and professional responsibility in future lawyers (Sousa Santos, 2012; García-Añón, 2017). Moreover, in a time when universities are being transformed into transnational institutions within the global market, it is important to show students that this global market has very different power relations behind the distribution of its cost and benefits, that affect people quite diversely depending on their personal circumstances. Accordingly, when we encourage students to adopt a critical approach to the knowledge they receive, we must show them that they can use it as a public good and not only as a commodity to compete in a globalized world. A sort of rebellious lawyering attitude for detaching themselves from the reality that is regularly provided to them in the lecture room, and look beyond it in order to progress towards equality and social justice (Harkavy, 2006; Brooks & Madden, 2011/12).

The second area in which it is relevant to look into is the capacity of the university to reproduce and disseminate an Eurocentric view of the world "a view powerful enough (in both intellectual and military terms) to claim universal validity" (Sousa Santos, 2016). Hence, the relevant question here is to know if the university is prepared to detach itself from the Westernized view of the world that promotes and structures visible and invisible patterns of hierarchy, domination, and discrimination (Kennedy, 1982). Moreover, this is in a time where different religions, moral concepts, collective identities and political visions are present in Europe. It is a breeding ground used by many political parties to link diversity with the aversion to difference (Baliabar, 2006), resulting in the creation of new enemies which are useful to pursue the reproduction of this Eurocentric view of the world and its social values.

Given this reality, it is the time to make a determined effort to counteract all the above-mentioned challenges and to regain the academic freedom and social responsibility characteristics of the public university based on the promotion of equality and diversity within multicultural societies. The Bologna process underlined the social or third mission that public universities have, that is encouraging researchers to carry out projects which have the purpose of improving the life of citizens, especially of those who are put in a situation of vulnerability by the system.

Thereby, legal clinics that adopt a human rights model are academic communities where faculty members, students and civil society discuss about matters of social relevance and work together to create a more inclusive society forcing the above-mentioned boundaries of the law (García-Añón, 2011, 2013; Mestre-i-Mestre, 2018). This is a community where everybody learns. On the one hand, the training of the students benefits from direct contact with the problems of society. It is a unique way to promote the critical vision of the legal order, for counteracting and unveiling the hierarchy and power structures present in our societies, that expel from the system sectors of the population based on direct and indirect discriminatory behavior. Students have to realize that the law is the result of a political process. Policy responds to certain objectives and values, regularly mentioned and protected in our Constitutions, but also subjected to distortions by the power of laissez-faire capitalism and globalization (Dunkan, 2016). And here is where students have to question the legitimacy behind the decisions adopted by law-makers and the resulting regulations themselves. This learning context is strongly encouraged in legal clinics (Gascón-Cuenca, 2016; 2018).

Therefore, the above-mentioned activities suggest students to research, recognize and reveal unmet legal needs that are not covered by the legal aid services (Owen, 2017). As noted in section number two, access to justice is a basic human right in a society that bases its social relations on conflict, because it allows people to fight for their rights in court. Legal Clinics base their roots in their local communities. By doing so, students are more prone to understand the reality that surrounds them by including themselves as another operator working on the case. By performing this task, the students are able to contextualize the juridical knowledge they learnt during the law degree, use it in real cases, and critically observe how the justice system works. From our experience, this process has proved fruitful in revealing to students the disparities people suffer, not only in the recognition of their rights, but also when claiming their protection in a court of law. The lack of equality of arms mentioned above.

Accordingly, the Legal Clinic for Social Justice of the University of Valencia, and the Clinic Prison and Right I of the University of Turin, are firmly committed to the development of projects aiming to achieve the objectives mentioned in the previous paragraphs. Both actively work with civil society actors and individuals from the groups that have suffered the worst consequences of the drastic financial cutbacks, or cases situated on the borders of the law. By doing so, we request students to put into practice the aforementioned abilities and the skills in order to promote social justice. We have been developing projects that directly affect our local communities (García-Añón, 2011, 2013, 2018; Gascón-Cuenca, 2016, 2018; Gascón-Cuenca et. al. 2018; Fernández-Artiach et. al., 2017). From this experience, we identified similar needs in both social contexts. It brought our work together and we start to actively collaborate to benefit from the exchange of expertise and abilities.

Universities, legal clinics and law students have a crucial leading role in overcoming the pitfalls explained in this piece of research, not only when it comes to the recognition and protection of human rights, but also in the battle of shaking the boundaries of the law to create a more equal and inclusive society, reinforcing the importance of the constitutional values protected by our Fundamental Charters.

Final remarks

Finally, as it has been shown, the crisis that hit Spain and Italy was not only financial but it was a crisis of values that severely affected our welfare systems, having a major impact on people in a position of vulnerability. Even though both States have signed international agreements that protect access to justice as a core human right due to its importance as a multidimensional key right, its guarantees have been seriously curtailed. As a consequence, sectors of the population that fall short of the low means and merit tests imposed for being eligible for free legal advice services, struggle to fight for their rights in court, as policymakers have left aside proportionality checks in the determination of these thresholds. This has drawn important boundaries in the legal systems. Access to justice is not generally granted to all the population, independently of their economic status, but closely related to the litigants' economic power. In such a scenario, universities, legal clinics and law students play a fundamental role in trying to make a difference for those left behind by the legal system. One of the university's cornerstones is its commitment with civil society and, historically, it has been very actively involved in the fight for the recognition of rights. Consequently, now is the time to continue this battle in order to strive for a more inclusive society based on a formal and substantial protection of human rights.

References

Anderson, Joel & Axel Honneth. "Autonomy, Vulnerability, Recognition, and Justice", 127-149, in J. Christman & J. Anderson (Eds.), *Autonomy and the Challenges to Liberalism: New Essays.* Cambridge: CUP, 2004.

Añón-Roig, María José. "El acceso a la justiciar de las personas migrantes:

la asistencia jurídica gratuita" 287-318, in Javier de Lucas y Maria José Añón-Roig (Eds.). *Integración, inmigración y derechos: a la búsqueda de indicadores.* Barcelona: Icaria, 2013.

Añón-Roig, María José. "The Fight Against Discrimination and Access to Justice. A Path to Integration", *Migraciones Internacionales* 8-3 (2016): 222-255.

Añón-Roig, María José. "El derecho de acceso como garantía de justicia: perspectivas y alcance", 19-76, in Cristina García-Pascual (Ed.), *Acceso a la justiciar y garantía de los derechos en tiempos de crisis.* Valencia: Tirant lo Blanch, 2018.

Baliabar, Étienne. "Strangers as Enemies: Further Reflections on the Aporias of Transnational Citizenship" *Globalization Working Papers* 06/4 (2006): 1-17.

Bilbao Ubillos, Juan María. "La llamada *Ley Mordaza:* la Ley Orgánica 2/2015 de protección de la seguridad ciudadana", *Teoría y Realidad Constitucional* 36(2015): 217-260.

Brooks, Susan L. & Robert G. Madden. "Epistemology and Ethics in Relationship-Centered Legal Education and Practice", *New York Law School Law Review* 56 (2011-2012): 331-366.

Bondia Garcia, David. "La criminalización de la protesta frente al nuevo ciclo de protestas sociales: ¿Dónde quedaron los compromisos de derogación de la Ley Mordaza?, 90-120, in Manuela Mesa (Coord.), *Derechos Humanos y seguridad internacional: amenazas e involución.* Madrid: CEIPAZ, 2018.

Cromwell, Thomas A. "Access to justice: towards a collaborative and strategic approach". *The Free Library* January-1 (2012). Accessed August 2018: https://www.thefreelibrary.com/Access to justice: towards a collaborative and strategic approach.

Del Carpio Fiestas, Verónica. "Justicia para el que pueda pagarla. Un alegato contra las tasas con ejemplos de procesos civiles de consumo" *Revista CESCO de derecho de consumo* (2012): 87-98.

De Sousa Santos, Boaventura. "La Universidad en el Siglo XXI. Para una reforma democrática y empancipadora de la Universidad", 139-194, in René Ramírez (Coord.), *Transformar la Universidad para Tranforma la Sociedad.* Quito: SENESCYT, 2012.

De Sousa Santos, Boaventura. "The University at a Crossroads", 3-14, in Ramón Grosfoguel, Roberto Hernández and Ernesto Rosen Velásquez (Eds.), *Decolonizing the Westernized University.* London: Lexington Books, 2016.

Esping-Andersen, Gøsta. *Fundamentos sociales en las economías postindustriales.* Barcelona: Ariel, 2000.

Fernández-Artiach, Pilar; Jose García-Añón; Ruth M. Mestre i Mestre. "Birth, growth and reproduction of Clinical Legal Education in Spain", 145-154, in Richard Grimes (Ed.), *Re-imagining legal education under the civil and common law.* London: Routledge, 2017.

Ferraris, Valeria. "L'accesso alla giustizia", 107-118, in Stefano Anastasia, Valentina Calderone, & Lorenzo Fanoli (Eds.), *L'articolo 3. Primo rapporto sullo stato dei diritti in Italia.* Roma: Edisse, 2014.

FRA. *Handbook on European Law Relating access to Justice*, Luxemburg: FRA, 2016.

Francioni, Francesco. "The Rights of Access to Justice under Customary International Law", in Francesco Francioni, *Access to Justice as a Human Right.* Oxford: OUP, 2007.

García-Añón, Jose. "El aprendizaje cooperativo y colaborativo en la formación de los jueces y juristas" *Revista de Educación y Derecho. Edutaction and Law Review* 4 (2011): 1-22.

García-Añón, Jose. "Transformation in Legal Teaching and Learning: Clinical Legal Education as a Transformative Component" (2013), 16, in J García-Añón (Ed.) *Transformaciones en la Docencia y Enseñanza del Derecho. Actas del V Congreso Nacional de Docencia en Ciencias Jurídicas.* Unitat d'Innovació Educativa – University of Valencia.

García-Añón, Jose. "Teaching and learning legal ethics and professional responsibility under the civil law", 96-103, in Richard Grimes (Ed.), *Re-thinking legal education under the civil and common law.* Routledge: London, 2017.

García-Añon, Jose. "Acceder a la justiciar y hacer justiciar: la función de las universidades, las clínicas jurídicas y las ong, y su impacto construyento los límites del derecho", 301-328, in Cristina García-Pascual (Ed.), *Acceso a la justiciar y garantía de los derechos en tiempos de crisis.* Valencia: Tirant lo Blanch, 2018.

Gascón-Cuenca, Andrés. "The Evolution of the Legal Clinical Methodology at the Spanish Universities: opportunities and challenges posed by the Strategic Litigation at the Human Rights Clinic" *Revista de Educación y Derecho. Education and Law Review* 14 (2016): 1-15.

Gascón-Cuenca, Andrés. "Clínica Internacional de Derechos Humanos" (2018), 45-52, in Ruth Maria Mestre-i-Mestre (Ed.) *Guía práctica para la enseñanza del Derecho a través de las Clínica Jurídicas.* Valencia: Tirant lo Blanc, 2018.

Gascón-Cuenca, Andres; Carla Ghitti & Francesca Malzani. "Acknowledging the relevance of empathy in Clinical Legal Education. Some proposals from the experience of the University of Brescia (IT) and Valencia (ESP)". *International Journal of Clinical Legal Education*, 25 (2018b), 218-247.

Guillén, Ana M.; Sergio González-Begega & David Luque Balbona. "Austerity and social retrenchment in Southern Europe. The fragmentation of the Mediterranean welfare model", *Revista Española de Sociología* 25-2 (2016): 261-272.

Harkavy, Ira. "The role of universities in advancing citizenship and social justice in the 21st century", *Education, citizenship and social justice* 1-1(2006): 5-37.

Hemerijck, Anton. *Changing Welfare States*. Oxford: OUP, 2013.

Juan-Sánchez, Ricardo. "Calidad de la justiciar, gestión de los tribunales y responsabilidades públicas: algunos estándares internacionales y otras buenas prácticas para favoreces el acceso a la justicia", 77-134, in Cristina García-Pascual (Ed.), *Acceso a la justiciar y garantía de los derechos en tiempos de crisis*. Valencia: Tirant lo Blanch, 2018.

Kennedy, Duncan. "Legal Education and the Reproduction of Hierarchy", *Journal of Legal Education* 32 (1982): 591-615.

Lloredo, Álix, Luis. "Derechos y democracia: juntos pero no revueltos", in Hugo Seleme, Guillermo Lariguet, Oscar Pérez de la Fuente y René González de la Vega (Eds.), *Democracia: perspectivas políticas e institucionales*. Montevideo-Buenos Aires: Editorial B de F, 2019.

Martínez Sánchez, César. "Una aproximación crítica a las tasas judiciales desde el derecho financiero y tributario", *RJUAM* I (2013): 205-221.

Mestre-i-Mestre, Ruth Maria "Aprender y dar sentido a enseñar el derecho. Filosofía jurídica y enseñanza clínica del derecho", 251-270, in Javier de Lucas, Ernesto Vidal, Encarnación Fernández & Vicente Bellver (Cords.) *Pensar el tiempo presente. Homenaje al professor Jesús Ballesteros Llopart*. Valencia: Tirant lo Blanch, 2018.

Mestre-i-Mestre, Ruth Maria. "Desalojos de hogares que no son casas. Derechos sociales y acceso a la justicia de colectivos marginalizados", 171-200, in Cristina García-Pascual (Ed.), *Acceso a la justiciar y garantía de los derechos en tiempos de crisis*. Valencia: Tirant lo Blanch, 2018.

Moreno, Luis. "La «vía media» española del modelo de bien estar mediterráneo", *Papers* 63/64 (2001): 67-82.

Owen, Richard. "Lawzone: Mapping Unmet Legal Need", *International Journal of Legal Clinical Education* 24-2 (2017): 3-42.

Ridaura Martínez, María Josefa, "La reforma del artículo 135 de la Constitución española: ¿Pueden los mercados quebrar el · consenso constitucional?", *Teoría y Realidad Constitucional* 29 (2012): 237-260.

Rodríguez Cabrero, Gregorio, "La fragmentación del régimen de bienestar Mediterráneo", *Revista Española de Sociología* 25-2 (2016): 273-276.

Ruiz Garijo, Merdeces. "La banalidad de las tasas judiciales: una nueva fractura del estado de bienestar" *Nueva Fiscalidad* 1 (2013): 9-40.

Santoro, Emilio. "«Una beffa alla sua miseria»: precondizioni dell'effettività del diritto ad avere diritti" *Ragion Pratica* 2 (2014): 435-454.

Trapella, Francesco. «L'empirica nozione di "famiglia" nel t.u. sulle spese di giustizia», *Processo Penale e Giustizia* 2 (2013): 69-74.

UN. *United Nations Principles and Guidelines on Access to Legal Aid in Criminal Justice Systems*. New York: UN, 2013.

Van de Meene, Ineke & Benajmin van Rooji. *Access to Justice and Legal Empowerment*. Leiden: Leiden University Press. 2008.

José García-Añón[1]

Access to Justice and the Impact of the European Legal Clinics in Case Law[2]

Introduction

The main focus of this paper is on the role of NGOs, legal clinics and universities in building the law and the case law using their own contribution to the case law on access to justice as an example. This paper considers how these entities are expanding the borders of the law in regard to the concept of access to justice.

So that, this paper takes a "broad conception" of access to justice. Access to justice is defined in the context of recognition of citizenship rights and examining proposals designed to objectify and measure its elements. Access to justice should involve not just the right to have rights, but access to their effective recognition and guarantee. Access to justice is a fundamental right, although not specifically recognised in all international treaties.

This piece of research considers the new functions undertaken by NGOs, universities and legal clinics in building the boundaries of law delimiting the concept of access to justice, particularly through looking at the means of access to justice and rights, primarily through *amicus* third-party intervention in court cases.

Moreover, this text describes the impact of these entities on defining the bounds of access to justice. This includes a discussion of the need for better

1   Human Rights Institute. University of Valencia (Spain).

2   I would like to thank Leah Wortham (Columbus School of Law of the Catholic University of America), Paula Galowitz (New York University Law School), Catherine F. Klein (Columbus School of Law of the Catholic University of America), and Lisa Radtke Bliss (Georgia State University) for reading, reviewing and comment this text. I am sure their constructive criticism and advices have made the text easier to read.

information on such impact and the complexity of framing research for such measurement. Some assessment of the impact on ECtHR case law is included.

What role can "other actors" have if legal aid is almost universal? How can the quality of access to justice be improved in the context of limited funding of public services? The following sections address these questions in several ways including the role of other actors in constructing legal legitimacy. Regarding lawyers and pro bono activities, the article explores that they may be an answer in the limited resource context but also an opportunity for lawyers to take responsibility in guaranteeing rights. The important role that clinical legal education programs can play through mechanisms such as intervention as third parties is explored. Such activities on the one hand reinforce collaboration with bar associations and NGOs and on the other by building the boundaries of law. The paper finally considers the broad sense of access to justice incorporating more than lawyer's participating in litigation, e.g., giving information, advice, and other types of assistance than court action.

The growing concern about what is called an *access to justice approach* means that our legal systems tend are interested in the needs of those who have the most difficulty in claiming their rights (Garth & Cappelletti, 1978: 278) and consideration of mechanisms to make this access possible. This includes consideration of the transformation of the role of courts when creating "new" human rights guarantees to protect excluded groups, particularly vulnerable populations, those who require special protection, or fall otherwise outside the "usual" sphere of protection of justice. (Gargarella et al, 2006; Abramovich, 2010)

A concept of integral justice should be employed based on the evolution of the concept of access to justice taking into account the various aspects of justice (distributive, retributive and restorative).

In several papers, I have proposed rethinking the classic evolution of stages of the concept of access to justice proposed by Garth and Cappelletti (Garcia Añón, 2014c, 2017a, 2017b.) It could be said that the first stage of this evolution is reduced to the concept of retributive justice. In the second wave, it includes and pays attention to distributive justice. Finally, from the third wave, there is a greater emphasis on restorative justice. This vision not only allows us to better define the concept of justice but also respond to some of the problems that arise in each of the areas.

International practice reveals an expansion of the concept of the right of access to justice by including cases where is not explicit, as well as a delimitation of its scope in reference to other interests and objectives of the public sphere (Francioni, 2007: 33 and ff).

The objective is to analyze how citizens can better demand their rights, understanding access to justice in a broad sense. This incorporates forms of participation in public life, here within the judicial system, as an element that provides legitimacy to the legal and political system.

Cappelletti and Garth's proposal on the evolution of the modern concept of access to justice after World War II can be used to understand where are we today. The description through waves is incomplete and used in an explanatory way. The waves show trends in the changing concept of "justice".

Garth and Cappelletti's "third wave" posits a broader conception of access to justice through encompassing a variety of alternatives to litigation to resolve conflicts and justice problems, as well as reforms to simplify justice systems and facilitate greater accessibility through public information on judicial procedure. (Garth & Cappelletti 1978: 222 and ff.)

This broader, more comprehensive conception of access to justice or this access-to-justice approach involves changes in the conception of what is included in the idea of justice (What?), the forms of access (How?), and the recipients (Who?).

Using this framework, the paper describes changes in the role of "other actors" and their countribution in building law, particularly the role of legal clinics in expanding the borders of the law on access to justice in Europe.

Garth & Cappelletti Waves Reviewed

		What *Standards*	*How*	*Who* *recipients*	*Who* *participate*
First Wave	*Free legal aid for disadvantaged people*	Providing access to legal representation in the courts for the economically disadvantaged	Legal aid service on representation at trial for persons accused of crimes	Individual case-advocacy /economically disadvantaged.	Bar associations/ Legal aid
Second Wave	*The representation of diffuse interests*	Right to legal representation on groups, public interest law…: poor as class, consumers, environmental rights…	Class actions, public interest actions (*test case*, public interest litigation…)	Groups and collective rights.	Public interest lawyers, Legal clinics
Third Wave	*Broad conception of access to justice*	To resolve disputes and justice problems Solving problems: satisfaction of needs Restorative justice	Development of alternatives to litigation in court: community mediation, victim-offender reconciliation and court-based mediation Simplify justice system, accessibility	Change of roles; victims.	Solve problems in a multidisciplinary manner. *New actors or new roles of the traditional actors.*

Access to Justice and Access to Rights: An Integral Approach.

The concept of access to justice needs a holistic approach to connect what has been described above as the third wave (Currie, 2004: 2 and 11). This is not a question of different stages, but rather of different moments in which it is assumed what had been achieved in the previous stages. This approach implies changes in the standards of justice, the forms of access to justice and the role of the various actors involved in legal disputes.

The Standards of Justice. (What is it?)

Justice should focus on solving problems. This involves not just compliance with the law but also the search for a solution that is satisfactory to all parties concerned (Currie, 2004: 14). Here, the concept of restorative justice is fully incorporated as a form of response in which the individual is reintegrated into the community or reconciled with the victim. It is not a question of replacing traditional systems of conflict resolution but rather of combining with them. The aim is to solve problems in an interdisciplinary way rather than just applying the law. It is not only a matter of guaranteeing the rights of individuals, but also of paying attention to their needs (Currie, 2004: 2 and 11).

In addition, as we will see below, one of the aspects that would identify the broad concept of access to justice would be opening the process to broad participation by actors who do not have a direct interest and are participating from a "public interest" perspective.

The extension and incorporation of what must be part of justice, e.g., to interests and needs, extends the traditional concepts used in the legal field. For example, discrimination is transformed and opens the possibility to multiple discrimination or intersectionality in the case we are faced with two or more sources of discrimination that combined give rise to a situation of inequality qualitatively different from the sum of the parts or forms of discrimination considered separately" (Añón, 2010, 2013a, 2013b: 151). As Barrère says: "The intersectional perspective of discrimination forces a revision of classical anti-discriminatory law based on the juxtaposition of discrimination factors." (Barrère, 2010: 251; Mestre, 2006, 2010a, 2010b).

Means of Access to Justice (How?)

Given the inadequacy of the institutionalized system of justice, in which many of the conflicts that arise have economic or social dimensions that the judicial system is unable to solve, other mechanisms may be effective in achieving real economic, social and cultural rights (Garth & Cappelletti, 1978: 184-185). In most US and some European jurisdictions, low-income people do not meet the requirements to qualify for free legal advice and are unable to afford a lawyer. At the same time, there is a decline of support for state-sponsored legal aid (Cummings & Sandefur, 2013: 87-88). Accordingly, "legal needs and challenges in society continue to grow, and the gap between those needs that are met and those that are unmet also continues to increase." (Blaze & Morgan, 2013: 196). What strategies can be developed to promote access to justice? Who can, and should, provide meaningful assistance in helping to bridge those gaps and provide real access to justice, and how can they do it? (Blaze & Morgan, 2013: 182); and, how can society exercise and enjoy of rights and justice if institutional mechanisms are insufficient and structural reform becomes complex? Answers to these questions imply promoting the guarantee of rights in procedures that are not court-centered and proposing new forms of problem-solving and negotiation. For example, one of the issues is to develop alternative dispute resolution means (mediation, arbitration... etc.) or the complementary means of access to justice (clinical legal education, pro bono activities.....), the viability of their institutionalization through norms and the effectiveness standards or the difficulties of assessing the effectiveness of these means.

The use of alternative means to facilitate access to justice is recommended in all reports and protocols detailing indicators of access to justice as objective instruments to measure effectiveness. (European Commission 2013, 2014: 20; FRA, 2011).

Increasing access to justice involves examining both formal and informal means:

a) The recognition of international standards of justice beyond the criteria established in each State;
b) The participation of civil society in justice through NGOs and other civil organizations;
c) The importance of training and education, including through legal clinics whose objective, in addition to training, includes making social justice effective in a global and international context (Bloch, 2011);
d) The importance of addressing the needs of vulnerable groups who are sometimes excluded from institutional procedures guaranteeing rights (Ikawa, 2011: 202).

Examples of increasing access to justice include the work of different non-governmental organizations and civil society that supports certain groups, such as immigrants or disabled people, and the work of Legal Clinics or pro bono lawyers.

Clinical Legal Education and Access to Justice

Clinical legal education (CLE) is more than a teaching methodology. It is defined as a space for active learning, in which law students' training experience is designed and planned, in a real or realistic context, in such a way that they are able to take responsibility for the outcomes of their learning through a process of reflection (García-Añón, 2014a, 2014b).

Clinical legal education is an important tool for the transformation of legal education, from three perspectives (Alvarez, Fernández, Grimes, Klein, Mestre & Wortham, 2013; García Añón, 2014b; García-Añón, 2014c). First, it calls for innovative teaching methods; second, it can serve the university's mission by working within and for society, beyond its role in teaching and research; and, third, it promotes access to justice and human rights.

The clinical methodology, as a space and time of learning, besides recovering some of the elements that require the teaching and learning of law today, is an element of social transformation, within what can be considered as the university social mission or function.

The main characteristics of clinical legal education that could support this "strategy" of transformation, would be the following: Learning from experience, training in professional skills, promoting the social function of university activity and understanding access to justice as an essential element of the guarantee of other rights.

From the perspective of participation of the actors in the process (*Who?*) this strategy implies a change in the current roles: the affected people, the accused and the victims must assume a more active role in the process of increasing access to justice. At the same time, the traditional roles of judges, prosecutors and lawyers should be reconsidered, as well as the roles of new actors who can be part of these processes in defense of the public interest and of civil society in general. An important aspect of this is to assess the impact of new actors (NGOs, universities...) on access to justice and the configuration of rights.

International and national standards diverge in the assumptions of the problem of determining evidence in cases of ethnic profiling by police (García Añón, 2014c; García Añón et a, 2013). NGOs play a role in promoting the case law of international bodies and impact domestic legal systems.

Who has an interest in doing justice? Third party actors can sometimes provide their legal point of view with a perspective that can be considered neutral in the process, or at least independent. For example, this process is addressed in Europe, articles 36 § 2 of the European Convention on Human Rights and article 44 § 2 (*Third-party intervention*) of the Rules of Court.

In recent years, the number of Spanish universities offering clinical legal education has been increased, developed and consolidated (Blázquez, 2011, Blázquez and García Añón, 2013). In the first wave, from 2003 to 2006, legal clinics appeared following a process of reflection on the introduction of active methodologies and their relationship to reality as a part of the innovation experience in the Bologna Process (the convergence process to the European Higher Education Area). The influence and relationship of Latin American clinics in the foundation and support of Spanish clinics was crucial (González et al., 2003; González, 2004; Blázquez, 2005; Villarreal and Courtis, 2007; Witker, 2007, CELS, 2008; Madrid, 2008, 2010; IIHR, 2011; RED, 2011). Following the new Degree in Law curricula in 2010, beginning around 2012, other universities implemented clinical legal education. This coincided with an increasing interest in pro bono activities among professionals. The development of this second wave was due to a number of factors. First, the existence of national networks exchanging experiences and good practices through national and international meetings on legal clinics. As in other countries and contexts, one of the priorities was to create a community of support, this is the setting up of a network of legal clinics to promote visibility and recognition by public institutions. Second, the development of training materials. And finally, the implementation in 2010-2011 of new degree in law curricula required the development of active methodologies and clinical methods satisfied this requirement.

The Impact of NGOs and Legal Clinics Activity in the Case Law

Compared with other legal systems, in Europe we have fewer studies and information on the impact of the work of other actors building the boundaries of law. Also, unlike other jurisdictions all over the world, in the case of many European countries coverage of access to justice through free legal aid is higher. In the case of USA, "Federally-funded legal services, at best, serve less than twenty percent of the legal need". Finally, the effort and impact of complementary means of access to justice (pro bono, Universities, NGOs ...) is greater in countries like USA: "The pro bono efforts of private attorneys supplement the work of the legal aid offices. But even legal aid and pro bono efforts combined only serve twenty per cent of the civil legal needs of the poor" (Blaze and Morgan, 2013:182).

It may be difficult to demonstrate with certainty that a ruling or a change in a government's policy was the direct result of strategic litigation or an activity developed by a NGO or a legal clinic. There are practical challenges in measuring success, including an absence of baseline data, failure to collect statistics, and lack of data analysis.

It is a fact, however, that in the last decades, clinical legal experiences available to law students have grown enormously all over the world (Bloch, 2011). This is undoubtedly true in Europe and particularly in Spain. (Bartoli, 2016; Fernández-Artiach, García-Añón and Mestre, 2017).

Research, studies and surveys about the impact of CLE on Legal Education reveal its aims: (Blázquez & García-Añón, 2013; García-Añón, 2014c, 2014d)

1) To reduce deficiencies in traditional legal education: how CLE can help to improve practical and professional instruction; skills acquisition; legal ethics and professionalism, and developing a social justice ethos among law students.
2) To enhance the social dimension of University ("The civic dimension"): by working with public interest organizations or in pro bono activities.
3) To enhance the corporate social responsibility values of private sector organisations.
4) To assist in meeting the legal needs of under-represented clients and groups: "the social justice mission" of lawyers (Bloch, 2011).
5) To show how the Clinical Legal Education movement is global: "There are clinical programs at law schools all over the world, and clinical law teachers have been meeting together regularly at international conferences for many years" seeking to improve both the profession and legal academia (Bloch, 2011).

However, connected to this there is an impact on the Legal System that has not been deeply studied. How this impact can be measured?

1) First, the impact on the public legal aid service. Europe does not have comprehensive research about legal aid. However, in the USA, there is some data with "extrapolation from recent surveys yield[ing] an estimate of 2.4 million hours of legal services provided annually by civil (1.8 million hours) and criminal (600,000 hours) clinics (…)The report's authors estimate almost 90,000 clients are represented in civil matters (including group clients counted as one each) and more than 38,000 clients in criminal cases" (2007-2008 Survey) (Cited in Sandefur & Selbin 2009:60, n.8).

Which is the potential impact in the terms of work commitment? For example, if 120 students devote about 205 hours of legal work per semester in a six-credit clinical course and 7 faculty members expend over 300 hours of supervision per semester, the number of hours devoted by students and faculty would be around 20.000. That is the equivalent of ten full-time lawyers (Blaze and Morgan, 2013: 184).

In a 2002 essay, David Luban calculated that students in US clinical courses produced three million hours of legal services for the poor each year: "These assumptions… imply 7,500 clinical students per semester, each contributing 200 hours of indigent representation, for a total of 1.5 million hours, or three million hours in an academic year" (Luban, 2003: 246 n.108).

In addition to clinical courses, most law schools also have pro bono programs: "One hundred seventy-six of the nearly 200 law schools in this country are listed in the 2011 Directory of Law School Public Interest and Pro Bono Programs disseminated by the ABA's Standing Committee on Pro Bono and Public Service and the Center for Pro Bono. Of these 176 law schools, 21 law schools have a pro bono graduation requirement, 118 have a formal voluntary pro bono program, and 19 have independent, student pro bono group projects" (Blaze & Morgan, 2013: 187).

So, the potential to promote greater access to justice through clinics and pro bono is considerable. Presently, this is not the case in Europe. Besides we have not enough information, except in the cases of the UK and Poland.

A recent report from the UK shows an increase in the number of clinics and cases compared to the previous years: "In the year April 2015 to March 2016, there were over 53,000 enquiries at clinics, with over 35,000 clients receiving legal advice and nearly 11,000 given information, signposting or referral". 71% of clinics have seen an increase in the number of clients in crisis or distress. The most common areas in which advice is given across the clinics network, representing over half of all advice provided, are: family law 21%, employment 17.4%, housing 17.1%, asylum and immigration 14%, consumer and contract law 8%, civil litigation 5%, crime 2.6%, welfare benefits 2.4%, debt 2.2%. In total, 84.642 pro bono hours were volunteered. Students deliver the greatest number of hours (57%), and solicitors and barristers represent nearly a third of all hours (32%). 85% of clients had an annual income below the minimum income standard and 57% of clients accessing clinics are from ethnic minorities (LawWorks, 2016: 3, 10, 26).

A report from the *Polish Legal Clinics Foundation* showed 10,693 cases were submitted to 22 legal clinics between October 2014 to June 2015. 32 % (3383 cases) dealt with civil law problems. 1988 students and 351 supervisors worked at the clinics (Source: Polish Legal Clinics Foundation, http://www.fupp.org.pl).

2) Second, there is an implicit aspect in the promotion of access to justice to be measured. Clinical legal education promotes access to justice in different ways (assessment, awareness, legal literacy, etc,) as a complement to the institutional forms of access to justice and legal aid.

3) Legal clinics cover a diverse range of legal areas, including housing, consumer, family, employment, health and social care, immigration, asylum, human trafficking …, providing an advice-only service or advice and representation. This activity is useful to capture original empirical data and observe social phenomena that can be translated into policy impact about the limits of legal aid

or access to justice. Said in other words: it shows the aspects in which legal system is not working.

4) University law clinics also constitute a unique environment in which to test and develop innovative solutions to legal problems (Drummond & McKeever, 2015).

5) Last, the impact changing the meaning and "boundaries" of Law: why? Because most of these cases are in the limits of law, usually are outside the institutional system We could name some of them as "terminally ill" cases: they are "lost causes" or they don't have a chance (because lawyers cannot make money with them) and by this reason they are used by universities and NGOs, not just as an opportunity to learn, but to force the concept and the answer that law gives to real problems. You can see developed some of them related to ethnic and racial discrimination (García-Añón, 2012, 2013, 2014c, 2016) or disability or LGTB rights (Vanhala, 2009; Hodson 2013).

Among other issues, this activity benefits extending access to justice. Either because of the problems related to the prohibitions on matters reserved for the legal profession and are off-limits in legal services programs or because they are matters that may not interest a lawyer because of their lack of economic importance. For example, class action, public interest and other impact litigation.

Mapping Third-party Interventions before the ECtHR

Written comments can be submitted before the ECtHR by 'any State or person concerned not party to the proceedings' (Article 36 of the European Convention of Human Rights[3] and article 44 of the Rules of Court): entities, groups or individuals with relevant specialist legal expertise or factual knowledge. *Amicus curiae* have several functions, but I am focusing on "the role of representation of the public interest" and contribution "to the institutional legitimacy of courts" raising the attention of public opinion (Van den Eynde, 2013: 274-275). In fact, "the principal objectives pursued by the groups are to challenge national laws, practices and interpretations, to establish precedents, to inform and influence the Court and to extend the interpre-

---

3 "(1) In all cases before a Chamber or the Grand Chamber, a High Contracting Party one of whose nationals is an applicant shall have the right to submit written comments and to take part in hearings. (2) The President of the Court may, in the interest of the proper administration of justice, invite any High Contracting Party which is not a party to the proceedings or any person concerned who is not the applicant to submit written comments or take part in hearings and (3) In all cases before a Chamber or the Grand Chamber, the Council of Europe Commissioner for Human Rights may submit written comments and take part in hearings".

tation given to the Convention." (Van den Eynde, 2011, 2013: 275). While third-party interveners are supposed to be neutral, such submissions provide an opportunity to broaden the scope of analysis of rights and advance case law, provide information and set out questions of Law.

Although little information is available on amicus curiae submissions in the ECHR, or about their patterns and effects, the best source of information is a 2013 PhD dissertation by Van Den Eynde (2013). It shows some results of an empirical quantitative work about third-party interventions[4] (*amicus curiae*) in the ECHR (1986-2013). Besides some information can be extracted from a qualitative survey among 20 NGOs active before the ECHR (Van den Eynde, 2011). Interaction between advocacy groups and the European Court of Human Rights and the role this participation plays in the enforcement and development of human rights has an effect on the enforcement and development of human rights.

In research about 30 years of ECHR decisions, 294 briefs were found submitted in 237 cases (Van den Eynde, 2013:279 and ff; Cichowski, 2016) There has also been an increase of participation in the last years: "Looking to other global legal regimes that include a court or tribunal one can observe a gradual spread in advocacy group participation. Individuals and groups are now granted access through amicus curiae procedures to the international criminal tribunals (ICTY, ICTR) and the International Criminal Court:" (Cichowski, 2016).

The percentage of cases in which an intervention has been permitted is low: 1.3 per cent of the 17,000 judgments. The percentage, however, was greater in Grand Chamber cases. "The Grand Chamber has delivered 307 judgments in total and saw NGOs' intervention in 65 of them – that is in 21 per cent of cases" (Van den Eynde, 2013: 280). The Grand Chamber "has a special role in safeguarding a unified interpretation of the Convention and preventing risks of inconsistency among judgments." (Van den Eynde, 2013: 280). Interviews conducted with ECTHR judges suggest this participation plays a beneficial role in complex decisions by providing legal research and comparative perspectives to the dispute (Cichowski, 2016).

These numbers regarding *amicus* participation are low in comparison with the U.S. Supreme Court or the Inter-American Human Rights system, with their different culture and tradition of participation. (Van den Eynde, 2013: 281). A significant number of interventions are made jointly and involve repeat-players before the Court: 142 different NGOs/entities have been identified and 5 of them are law school clinics.

Since 2011, there have been an increasing number of interventions from

---

4   This includes any kind of non-profit associations (NGOs, law school clinics and research centres).

legal clinics in Europe, particularly from Spain, France, and Italy. It seems likely this trend will continue because one of the main activities of legal clinics is collaboration with other entities and non-governmental organizations submitting cases in international courts (Drummond & McKeever, 2015).

The characteristics that have been pointed out about the evolution in the concept of access to justice can be found in some of the issues that have recently been elucidated in the European system of protection of human rights. It could be found in features described in the second and third waves previously described. This is illustrated in the case *Beauty Solomon* (European Court of Human Rights, 24 july 2012, Application no. 47159/08). First, the importance of actors with public and indirect interests in the process (*who?* The content of the question refers to the participation of actors in the process). Second, how the use of instruments such as strategic litigation serves to advance in the decision-making within the ordinary spectrum of justice (*how?* That is, to determine what are the means of access to justice). Third, we can pay attention to the broad conception of access to justice, which is, through procedural aspects, linked to a broader vision of justice (which, in this case, is the multiple discrimination. Finally, the idea that equal treatment or non-discrimination continues to be one of the most violated aspects (*What?* The question is referred to the standards of justice).

Case *B.S. vs Spain* (ECHR, 24 July 2012)		
What	*How*	*Who*
Effective official investigation	Strategic Litigation	Third parties
Obligation to investigate, prosecute and punish their violations, or at least the most serious violations	Using the principle of shifting the burden of proof	The European Social Research Unit (ESRU), Research Group on Social Exclusion and Control (GRECS), Universidad de Barcelona, The AIRE Centre.
Discrimination access to justice/ Multiple discriminations		

Final Observations and Conclusive Remarks

What is the future of free legal services in European countries in which the provision of free legal services to needed people, through bar associations, is entrusted to private lawyers, but with public funding? I have not focused on the problems related to cost or quality (for example, requirements and training of lawyers). The main focus of this paper is to reflect about the role of other legal actors, the *others* (NGOs, Universities or legal clinics), along with the pro bono activities of lawyers, and their impact, not just in the courts' decisions but also in their role building the law or the case law, as part of the right of access to justice. This implies, as a consequence, a reflection about other tasks not strictly legal or procedural, but rather a focus on the political or social framework of our systems. In this sense, this paper focuses on the role of these *others*, different from the State, participating and taking part in searching a true right of access to justice.

The case of B.S. vs. Spain (ECtHR, 2012), described above, illustrates, as a trend, how a broad concept of access to justice can be detected based in a comprehensive approach of the idea of justice. From this perspective, this concept seeks not only to guarantee the rights of individuals but also the satisfaction of their needs or paying attention to other aspects, as victims.

This article proposes a broad concept of justice that has evolved incorporating the diverse aspects (restorative, distributive and retributive justice) and stresses the different perspectives in this evolution. Part of this approach answers the questions about *who*, *how*, and *what* is the idea of justice. This approach would imply changes in the role of the various actors involved in legal disputes, in the standards of justice, and in the forms of access to justice.

The increasing number of legal clinics in Europe should lead to an increase in actions, strategic litigation partnerships with NGOs and *amicus curiae* in the courts. Clinical legal education is an important player in using intervention as third parties in the procedure. It is shown how other unconventional mechanisms of access to justice are used, such as strategic litigation, which represents a way of advancing the requirement for decision-making. It is also observed how stakeholders in the process have no direct interest, which somehow constitutes a breach on the idea of traditional legal standing. This type of action will allow the discussion of issues and the modification of legal issues that are rigidly established by jurisprudence and which may have an impact on countries that are part of international conventions.

For example, as in the *Beauty Solomon Case*, the concept of effective official investigation together with the possibility of using the statistical test and shifting the burden of proof, once it has been prima facie established that there has been a serious infringement of a right, allows "doing justice" in a case of discrimination that would otherwise be impossible.

In summary, clinical legal education reinforces the collaboration with bar associations, civil society and other private and public institutions, and, at the same time, contributes to expanding the boundaries of law.

Obviously, although this is complementary of other public tasks related to legal aid, clinical legal education in collaboration with NGOs activities has to be taken into account, mainly because it can incorporate forms of participation in public life. In this case, in the jurisdictional system, it is an element that provides legitimacy to the legal and political system as a whole. This trend of presents theoretical and empirical challenges for future research.

References

Víctor Abramovich, "Responsabilidad estatal por violencia de género: comentarios sobre el caso "Campo Algodonero" en la Corte Interamericana de Derechos Humanos", *Anuario de Derechos Humanos,* 167-182 (2010). http://www.revistas.uchile.cl/index.php/ADH/article/viewFile/11491/11852

Alicia Álvarez, et al; "Legal Clinics as transformative components in the learning process: Teaching-learning methods and Legal Clinics models", *Transformaciones en la docencia y el aprendizaje del Derecho. Actas del Quinto Congreso Nacional de Docencia en Ciencias Jurídicas. Valencia, 11-13 de septiembre de 2013* (Jose García Añón, ed.),Unitat d'innovació educativa, Facultat de Dret, Universitat de València, 2013) www.uv.es/innodret/pub/2013actas_congreso.pdf

María José Añón-Roig, "Integración: una cuestión de derechos", *Revista Arbor,* 477 (2010): 625-638.

María José Añón-Roig, El acceso a la justicia de las personas inmigrantes: la asistencia jurídica gratuita, *Integración y derechos: a la búsqueda de indicadores*, (in De Lucas, Javier y Añón, María José eds., Barcelona: Ícara, 2013a).

María José Añón-Roig, "Principio antidiscriminatorio y determinación de la desventaja", *Isonomía, 39,* 127-157. (2013b)

Mª Ángeles Barrère Unzueta, "La interseccionalidad como desafío al *mainstreaming* de género en la políticas públicas", *Revista Vasca de Administración Pública*, 87-88/2010, 225-252: 2010.

Clelia Bartoli, "Legal Clinics in Europe: for a commitment of higher education in social justice", *Diritto & Questione Pubbliche*, May 2016.http://www.dirittoequestionipubbliche.org/page/2016_nSE_Legal-clinics-in-Europe/

DQ_2016_Legal-Clinics-in-Europe_specialissue.pdf

Douglas A. Blaze & R. Brad Morgan, "More equal access to justice: the unrealized potential of Law Schools", *Mississippi Law Journal*, (82) 181-197: 2013.

Diego Blázquez Martín, "Apuntes acerca de la educación jurídica clínica", *Universitas. Revista de Filosofía, Derecho y Política*, (3) 43-60: 2005/2006. http://universitas.idhbc.es/n03/03-04_blazquez.pdf Diego Blázquez Martín, "The Bologna process and the future of Clinical education in Europe", in *Frank Block ed., The Global Clinical Movement. Educating Lawyers for Social Justice*, New York, OUP,121-133, 2011.

Diego Blázquez Martín & J. García-Añón; Las Clínicas jurídicas españolas en el Movimiento Clínico Global, *El movimiento global de clínicas jurídicas. Formando Juristas en la Justicia social*, 11-22. (Frank S. Bloch, ed. Tirant lo Blanch, Valencia, 2013)

Frank S. Bloch (ed.), *The Global Clinical Movement. Educating Lawyers for Social Justice*, New York, OUP, 2011.

CELS, *Litigio Estratégico y derechos humanos. La lucha por el derecho*, Buenos Aires, Siglo XXI, 2008.

R.A. Cichowski, "The European Court of Human Rights, Amicus Curiae, and Violence against Women". *Law & Society Rev.*, 59 (2016) 890-919. Scott L. Cummings & Rebecca L. Sandefur, "Beyond the numbers: what we know –and should know- about american pro bono", *Harvard Law & Policy Review*, 7 (2013): 83-111.

Albert Currie, Riding the third wave: Rethinking Criminal Legal Aid within an Access to Justice Framework, *Research and Statistics Division*, (Department of Justice Canada, 2004) http://www.justice.gc.ca/eng/rp-pr/csj-sjc/ccs-ajc/rr03_5/rr03_5.pdf [access 8 june 2016]

O. Drummond & G. McKeever; *Access to Justice through University Law Clinics*, Ulster, Ulster University Law School, 2015.

http://www.ulster.ac.uk/lawclinic/files/2014/06/Access-to-Justice-through-Uni-Law-Clinics-November-2015.pdf

European Commission for the Efficiency of Justice, *The functioning of judicial systems and the situation of the economy in the European Union Member States. Compiled Report*, (Bruselles, European Commission, Directorate General Justice, 2013)

http://ec.europa.eu/justice/effective-justice/files/cepej_study_justice_scoreboard_en.pdf

European Commission, *The EU Justice Scoreboard. A tool to promote effective justice and growth. Communication from the Commission to the European Parliament, the Council, the European Central Bank, the European Economic and Social Committee and the Committee of the Regions, COM(2013) 160 final.*

http://ec.europa.eu/justice/effective-justice/files/justice_scoreboard_communication_en.pdf

European Commission, *The 2014 EU Justice Scoreboard, Communication from the Commission to the European Parliament, the Council, the European Central Bank, the European Economic and Social Committee and the Committee of the Regions, COM (2014)155 final*, Bruselles, European Commission, Directorate General for Justice, 2014.

http://ec.europa.eu/justice/effective-justice/files/justice_scoreboard_2014_en.pdf

Pilar Fernández-Artiach, et al, Birth, growth and reproduction of Clinical Legal Education in Spain, in *Richard Grimes ed., Re-imagining legal education under the civil and common law. A Road Map for Constructive Change*, London, Routledge, 145-154, 2017.

FRA (European Rights Agency for Fundamental Rights), *Access to justice in Europe: an overview of challenges and opportunities*, Luxembourg, Publications Office of the European Union, 2011.

http://fra.europa.eu/sites/default/files/fra_uploads/1520-report-access-to-justice_EN.pdf

Francesco Francioni, The Rights of Access to Justice under Customary International Law" in Francesco Francioni ed., *Access to Justice as a Human Right*, Oxford, OUP, 2007.

José García-Añón, Discriminación, exclusión social y conflicto en sociedades multiculturales: La identificación por perfil étnico, In Jose García Añon & Mario Ruiz Sanz eds., *Discriminación racial y étnica: balance de la aplicación y eficacia de las garantías normativas*, Valencia, Tirant lo blanc-Servei de Publicacions de la Universitat de València, 281-316, 2012.

José García-Añón, et al; *Identificación policial por perfil étnico en España. Informe sobre experiencias y actitudes en relación con las actuaciones policiales*, Valencia, Tirant lo Blanch-Publicacions de la Universitat de València, 2013.

http://www.uv.es/garciaj/pub/2013_perfil_etnico.pdf

José García-Añón, "Transformaciones en la docencia y el aprendizaje del Derecho: ¿La educación jurídica clínica como elemento transformador?", *Teoría y Derecho. Revista de Pensamiento Jurídico*, 15 (2014a): 12-33.

José García-Añón, "La integración de la educación jurídica clínica en

el proceso formativo de los juristas" *REDU. Revista de Docencia Universitaria*, número extraordinario "Formación de los licenciados en Derecho", 12-3 (2014b): 153-175.
http://red-u.net/redu/index.php/REDU/article/view/867

José García-Añón, "Access to justice and the guarantee of fundamental rights: international and domestic legal standards", *Citizen and State Structures. State and International Community, Citizen-state-international community. A collection of Studies, Part V, chapter 1,* 529-542 (eds. Kinga Flaga-Gieruszyńska, Ewelina Cała – Wacinkiewicz, Daniel Wacinkiewicz, Szczecin University/ C.H. Beck Publishing House, Warszawa,2014c)

José García-Añón, Acceso a la justicia y protección judicial efectiva: estándares en el Tribunal Europeo de Derechos Humanos sobre el alcance del derecho a un recurso efectivo, in Luis Efren Rios Vega-Irene Spigno dirs., *Estudios de casos líderes interamericanos y europeos. Vol. II. Problemas actuales de la Justicia regional. Una visión comparada entre América y Europa*, Saltillo, Tirant Lo Blanch, 2017a.

José García-Añón, El acceso a la justicia como garantía de los derechos humanos: apuntes sobre su evolución, *Pensar el tiempo presente. Libro Homenaje al Profesor Jesús Ballesteros*, Valencia, Tirant Lo Blanch, 2017b.

Roberto Gargarella, et al, *Courts and social transformation in new democracies: an institutional voice for the Poor?* London, Ashgate, 2006.

Bryant G. Garth & Mauro Cappelletti, "Access to Justice: The Newest Wave in the Worldwide Movement to Make Rights Effective", *Buffalo Law Review*, 27 (1978): 181-292.

F. González Morales et al; *Clínicas de Interés Público y Enseñanza del Derecho. Argentina, Chile, Colombia, México y Perú.* Cuadernos de análisis jurídico, 15, Centro de Derechos Humanos, Universidad Diego Portales, 2003.

F. González Morales, El trabajo clínico en materia de derechos humanos e interés público en América Latina, *Cuadernos Deusto de Derechos Humanos,* 27, Universidad de Deusto, 2004.

Instituto Interamericano de Derechos Humanos (IIDH), *Manual Autoformativo sobre acceso a la justicia y derechos humanos en Chile*, Instituto Interamericano de Derechos Humanos/Centro de Derechos Humanos de la Universidad Diego Portales de Chile/Instituto de Estudios Judiciales, San José de Costa Rica, 2011. *http://www.dere- choshumanos. udp.cl/wp- content/uploads/2012/12/aa.pdf*

L. Hodson, Activating the Law: Exploring NGOs' Legal Responses to Gross Human Rights Violations, *Making Human Rights Intelligible: Towards a Sociology of Human Rights.* 267-282 (M. R. Madsen, & G. Verschraegen (Eds.), Oxford: Hart. 2013).

Daniela Ikawa, The Impact of Public Interest Law on Legal Education, in Frank Block ed., *The Global Clinical Movement. Educating Lawyers for Social Justice*, New York, OUP, 2011.

David Luban, "Taking Out the Adversary: The Assault on Progressive Public-Interest Lawyers", *California Law Review,* 91 (2013).

Antonio Madrid, El acceso a los derechos: la experiencia del proyecto dret al Dret, *Anuario de Filosofía del Derecho*, 26 (2010): 31-56.

Antonio Madrid, El proyecto derecho al Derecho: un planteamiento de actuación y reflexión comunitario, in M. Martínez ed., *Aprendizaje, servicio y responsabilidad social de las universidades*, Barcelona, Octaedro, 2008.

Ruth Mestre i Mestre *La caixa de Pandora. Introducció a la teoría feminista del Dret*, (Tirant-Universitat de València 2006)

Ruth Mestre i Mestre, Mujeres, nueva ciudadanía y trabajo: ¿de qué mujeres hablamos?, in Maria Freixanet Mateo, coord., *Dones migrades treballadores. Anàlisi i experiències locals contra la desigualtat,* Barcelona, ICPS, 75-106, 2010a.

Ruth Mestre i Mestre Introducción a las teorías contemporáneas sobre identidad femenina y discriminación de género. in Cristina Monereo, *Género y derechos fundamentales, Granada*, Comares, 3.47, 2010b.

RED (Revista de Educación y Derecho/Education and Law Review), Monográfico "Clínica jurídicas: desafío y oportunidad", no 4, (2011)

http://revistes.ub.edu/index.php/ RED/issue/view/108

R. Sandefur & J. Selbin, "The Clinic Effect", *Clinical Law Review*, 16 (2009): 57-107.

http://scholarship.law.berkeley.edu/facpubs/225/

Laura Van den Eynde, Litigation Practices of Non-Governmental Organisations Before the European Court of Human Rights, *European Master's Degree in Human Rights and Democratisation: Awarded eses of the Academic Year 2009/2011*, Milan, Marsilio Editori, 2011.

Laura Van den Eynde, An Empirical Look at the Amicus Curiae Practice of Human Rights NGOs Before the European Court of Human Rights, *Netherlands Quarterly of Human Rights*, 31/3 (2013): 271-313.

LawWorks Clinics Network, *LawWorks Clinics Network Report April 2015-*

March 2016. Analysis of pro bono legal advice work being done across the LawWorks Clinics Network between April 2015 and March 2016, (2016,) (www.lawworks.org.uk) http://cort.as/-_ILi

Lisa Vanhala, "Anti-discrimination policy actors and their use of litigation strategies: the influence of identity politics", *Journal of European Public Policy,* 15-5 (2009): 738-754.

Marta Villarreal & Christian Courtis (Coord.); *Enseñanza Clínica del Derecho. Una alternativa a los métodos tradicionales de formación de abogados,* México, ITAM, 2007.

Jorge Witker, "La enseñanza clínica como recurso de aprendizaje jurídico" *Academia. Revista sobre enseñanza del Derecho,* 5-10 (2007): 181-207.

Jose Antonio García Sáez

Legal Clinics as a Training Methodology in Human Rights[1]

Introduction

In the Spanish-speaking world a large number of works have been published containing information on what the legal clinical methodology is and about its purpose[2]. One can also easily find material showing how appropriate this methodology is in particular for human rights education (González-Morales, 2003; or García-Añón, 2013). This text addresses issues related with the teaching of human rights not only as a specific course, but also as a cross-cutting theme of growing importance in contemporary law.

Firstly, we will briefly go over some values and skills that one can work on in a legal clinic. Values and skills that through the clinical methodology one can work on with students in a much more effective manner than with traditional teaching methods. Finally, considering the low presence of legal clinics in a country like Spain and the need to promote and develop them, three possible routes to introduce this learning method in law curricula will be suggested.

Values and Skills that can be Developed in a Legal Clinic

Clinical legal education breaks away from many of the forms that have been imposed for centuries in law faculties[3]. However, it does so using a

1 Human Rights Institute. University of Valencia (Spain). This work is part of the research projects Transformaciones de la justicia. Autonomía, inequidad y ejercicio de derechos" (DER2016-78356-P) and "Constitutional reform: philosophical and legal issues" (ref. DER2015-69217-C2-1-R), both financed by the Ministry of Economy, Industry and Competition.

2 Amongst others, Mestre i Mestre, 2008; Bloch, 2013; Torres Villarreal, 2015; Villarreal & Courtis, 2007; Witker, 2007; Blázquez Martín, 2006; or Molina Saldarriaga, 2008.

3 Duncan Kennedy (2014: 13), for example, has placed clinical legal education amongst

methodology that a priori may not seem very innovative: practice. The legal clinical methodology basically consists in practicing. It is based in the philosophy of learning by doing[4]. Indeed, for generations university teachers and particularly those who simultaneously have experience in the practice of law – lawyers, judges, public prosecutors, etc.—, have been aware of the importance of legal practice. Law has never been taught in a purely theoretical way, and cases, court petitions, forms or agreements have always been materials used in the training of future lawyers.

Nevertheless, the clinic introduces an essential element that students rarely had available until then: direct contact with clients. It is not a contact mediated by the law firm that they may be assisting in the internship that they have to do in order to finish their degree in Law, but a direct contact between the student and the client's necessities. What students have in front of them is a paramount challenge, finding of a solution –always supervised by a clinical teacher[5]– for the legal problems of the client. A question of taking responsibility of their work. We are not in front of the study of case-law that has already been solved. It is not a laboratory hypothesis. We are faced with a real case that students have to solve themselves. And the fate of the person who has placed himself or herself in our hands depends to a large extent on our performance, on us being able to do our best. So that, the value of responsibility is one of the greatest learning outcomes that students develop while working in the clinical environment[6].

Another characteristic of the clinic is its social impact. Generally, students work with clients that primarily belong to disadvantaged or excluded social groups, and they normally do not have the financial resources to pay for a high-level defence or cannot access to free and effective legal advice. Here is the reason why a legal clinic – and foremost those dealing with human rights cases– have to provide their services free of charge. The important issue lies in the criteria that will be used in the selection of cases and clients.

the subjects with the greatest emancipatory and critical potential.

4 A philosophy whose origins date back, at least, to Aristotle, who in his Nichomacean Ethics stated that "we become just with just acts, measured with measured acts, brave with brave acts" (2014: Book II, chapter I [1.103a, 1.10b]).

5 In the absence in Spain of a similar figure to the clinical teacher of the American universities, in this case reference to the "clinical university teacher" should be understood as one who collaborates and participates in the clinic, although the context —at least for the moment— makes a full time engagement in the clinic impossible, since this occupation has to be combined with the rest of the university teachers' duties.

6 For example, the declarations of the students of the Clínica Jurídica per la Justícia Social of the University of Valencia can be seen: https://www.youtube.com/playlist?list=PLdS-6zhURCt6B-I9ZqB-2eHXG0s2USfRw [Visited on 14th August 2018].

To that effect, it is important clarify some lines of work, that will have to match the fields of specialisation of the teachers or supervisors of the clinic as much as possible. We will look deeply into the practical aspects later on.

Before that, it is necessary to emphasise that working with these groups implies a window of opportunity to fulfil with the desirable transfer of knowledge that the university has to provide to society. Universities, at least the public ones, have to be at the service of the needs of society, and legal clinics are a mean through which these needs can directly reach this objective. Law students and lawyers in general have traditionally kept at a certain distance from the social problems that surrounded them. They are more concerned about solving the symptoms rather than seeking the causes of these problems, legal education has too often chosen to ignore the roots of social conflicts, thus not paying attention to the underprivileged groups. The contact with people who are part of these groups has been limited to social welfare or to public defenders. This new reality has shifted a new paradigm in the context of human rights. Accordingly, we start from the premise that human rights not only have to be learned but have to be comprehended (García-Sáez & Vanyó-Vicedo, 2015). This means that it is necessary to let oneself be imbued with social issues, be aware and observe at first hand which are some of the main human rights violations that occur in the world that surrounds ourselves. Once again, the legal clinic proves to be an unequalled instrument for such purposes, conferring a "reality check" to a certain student profile (and at times also to a certain teacher profile) that seems to live in a social bubble, isolated from the problems that affect large sections of the population on a daily basis. As Gascón-Cuenca *et al* (2018) have recently shown, the development of empathy plays a key part in this regard.

Moreover, a skill[7] that is invariably learned in a legal clinic is team-work. It is known to all that the work done by lawyers is a job that is carried out in collaboration with others colleagues, within a team. A good behaviour with co-workers, fluent communication, coordination and an efficient distribution of tasks, accepting criticism, or the amicable conflict resolution are aspects that have to do with team work and that are strengthened with the legal clinic. The student that goes through the clinic is aware that quality lawyering is always the result of team work. A work that requires coordination with others and that consequently demands the complementary development of values that have to do with coexistence and with respect for others, whatever their team role.

---

7 In the debate between the name skills or competencies, here it has been preferred to use the word skills which is consistent with basic legal rights, which were incorporated a long time ago in the curricula of Anglo-Saxon Law Schools and that gradually also start to be introduced in the curricula of continental faculties (Finch & Fafinsky, 2015; García-Añon, et al, 2008.

Thus, as the team work, there is another skill that is very important for a lawyer: leadership. Developing leadership capacity does not imply the establishment of rigid hierarchical organisational structures dominated by one or several more or less charismatic people who impose their rules on others. On the contrary, it implies encouraging the development of the capacities of each person, fostering self-confidence and, at the same time, awareness of one's limitations. Amongst the students of the clinic it is therefore positive to establish a shared and horizontal leadership; namely to assign responsibilities that have to do with different fields of work, showing young people that they are capable of leading a project or a part of it and being responsible for its outcome; while they acknowledge the authority of their co-workers in the area for which they are responsible. A good practice in this respect is the rotation of roles and responsibilities in the clinic. It is recommended that the students experiment in the different spheres that may exist within clinical work (client reception, interviews, research on cases, review of dossiers, site visits, case litigation, monitoring, management, media relations, institutional relations, etc.). It is equally recommended that the supervisor or coordinator of the clinic draws from his/her sensations and experiences so as to maximise the development of the capacity of each student, while optimising at the same time the results of the human group that establishes itself around the clinic.

An issue which is also linked with team work is interdisciplinarity. It allows us to claim once again that the methodology used in legal clinics is optimal for fomenting it. From work on real life cases one quickly realises that in actual fact there are virtually no exclusively criminal, administrative or civil law cases. This is even less so when approaching to a case or situation from a human rights perspective. Real life cases are not set out separately, as subjects have traditionally been taught in law faculties. On the contrary, they normally have implications that affect different areas of the legal system. And the lawyer has to be up to dealing with this complexity, determining, for example, the court of competent jurisdiction if he or she wants to litigate; or appropriately identifying the different implications of the case if one has the task of writing a report. In this way clinical practise puts to the test the knowledge gained by the student much better than any traditional exam. It is no longer only a matter of being acquainted with the provisions of the law, but also their application; and moreover, to apply them, jointly and simultaneously, fully running into the difficulties that characterise a dynamic and complete legal system, full of antinomies and gaps (Ferrajoli, 1999), that make the legal profession an exciting challenge.

Interdisciplinarity can also be understood as referring to the relationship of law with other areas of knowledge. In this regard one must say that the clinic highlights that lawyers are required to avail themselves of the assistance of other professionals when carrying out their work. Indeed, there is a long tradition in assistance from independent experts or criminologists specialised in the field of criminal law, in the same way in which the opinion of experts in evidence assessment during investigation and trial has always been essential. However, in clinical work on human rights, in a sphere in which we are working on sensitive issues that may imply a high degree of emotional involvement of the student, a tight collaboration with other students, for example psychology or social work ones, is recommended. Some experiences to this effect have been highly satisfactory, not only because better results have been obtained thanks to the visions brought by these other subjects, but because law students, in contact with students of other disciplines, gain a valuable learning experience with respect to the limitations that their law has for solving social problems. Not everything, as some lawyers seem to think, can be solved through courts of law, and students have to be aware of that.

The specific complexity to law practice frequently implies the appearance of many ethical conflicts. Legal clinics are a favourable space to work with students on criteria and instruments which will allow future professionals to solve these ethical conflicts in the most appropriate manner. This becomes important especially in a context like the Spanish one, in which ethics, as a subject, is forgotten or left aside often in the curricula of the great majority of Spanish faculties (García-Pascual, 2013). Insofar as clinical work is practical, and considering that usually it is the first time that students interact legal practice, it is essential to face this practice having established certain ethical criteria. For instance, given that the work we do is free of charge, should we accept the present that a grateful client offers us? If this was so, is any kind of present acceptable or would certain limits have to be set? What would the clinic have to do if —for example— a group turns to us with a well-founded claim against our own university, or else against another organisation whose funding depends on our university? How do we face the bad practices and vices that certain professionals in the world of the law consider normal, but still irregular? How far do the duties that we have towards our clients go? These and many other ethical conflicts arise each day in lawyers' practice, and starting practising the legal profession within the context of a legal clinic that relies on an adequate ethical perspective, is an unparalleled opportunity to train young law professionals committed to the culture of legality and the rule of law.

Moreover, it should be noted that the clinic is also about networking. For some decades, teachers dedicated to the clinic in different parts of the world have been devising what has come to be known as "global clinical movement"[8]. Moreover, similarly, networks of legal clinics have been established in different regions, such as Latin America[9], or at national level, such as the Spanish Universities' Legal Clinics Network[10]. These networks have been crucial for boosting the creation of new clinics in recent years and also to consolidate the existing ones, training teachers, sharing experiences and establishing mutual support links. Conferences like the one that the Global Alliance for Justice Education (GAJE) holds on biannual basis are an essential meeting point for law teachers worldwide that are committed to educating their students and to the service that they can provide to society.

Finally, the legal clinical method proves to be an optimal application of the new educational paradigms that place the student at the centre of the education process and not the teacher (Bain, 2005). Learning and not teaching, as educators claim, is what actually takes place in a clinic, in which the teacher takes on the role of moderator or supervisor, but not of professor, given that he/she is teaching his/her own practice of direct interaction with the client.

The Clinic in the Law Studies Curriculum

The change of paradigm that legal clinical education implies undoubtedly requires important efforts inside of the structures of the law faculties. It, not only calls for the education and training of its teachers, but also requires the adaptation of workspaces, where students can assemble, clients can be adequately assisted, dossiers can be stored safely, or phone calls can be made and received. However, if something is important for the operation and sustainability of a legal clinic over time, it is its introduction in the academic curriculum. There can be at least three complementary routes to implement the clinical methodology.

The first and main route is the one according to which the internships that all the students must usually carry out may be done in the legal clinic. This practical work –to which are normally assigned a specific number of credits– ensure that the student will follow a set timetable in the clinic, having to make an effort for its fulfilment, since it will be evaluated like any another subject. This enables to bring stability to the clinic, because the fact

---

8 The dissemination fostered for many years by the International Journal of Clinical Legal Education edited by the University of Northumbria is noteworthy: http://www.northumbriajournals.co.uk/index.php/ijcle [Visited on 14th August 2018].

9 http://www.clinicasjuridicas.org/ [Visited on 14th August 2018].

10 http://clinicas-juridicas.blogspot.com.es/[visited on 14th August 2018].

of having students that are carrying out their internships ensures that the cases may be duly dealt with, with staff that will necessarily have to devote hours of work to them. Similarly, the recognition of the curriculum facilitates faculty teachers' interest in getting involved in the clinic supervising and advising students in their work. One cannot disregard that a serious and rigorous supervision work puts a high demand on the teacher's time, and consequently such work has to be acknowledged in the curriculum in terms of recounting teaching hours. Likewise, the work of the person coordinating or directing the clinic must be acknowledged as management work. These acknowledgements by the faculty's administrative offices prove to be key elements for the establishment and success of a clinic (Giddings & Lyman, 2013; or García-Añón, 2014).

The ideal framework is the recognition in the curriculum of the clinic, room must also be given to those students who wish to join it voluntarily, as a complement to their education, or else as a route to satisfy personal concerns or legitimate feelings of solidarity towards the people that are assisted. In this respect examples of students who, after having carried out their compulsory internships in a clinic have wanted to remain as voluntary staff due to the high level of personal satisfaction provided by the experience are common. In any case, when it is voluntary work, the challenge for those in charge of the clinic is to create an environment that offers the necessary stimuli to create commitment amongst voluntary workers. On the contrary, there is the risk of leaving projects incomplete, clients unsatisfied and hopes unfulfilled.

The third route is its establishment within the different courses. The entire course or part of it may be perfectly assessed on the basis of the work carried out by students in a clinic. This being said, this route has some constraints. The first of these has to do with the necessary clinical education of the teaching staff. Accordingly, it is best to promote this kind of education from the faculty administrative offices, facilitating access to courses and workshops. The second constraint, on the other hand, is given by the size of the student groups and the specific faculty facilities. In general, it is difficult to establish a clinic with more than ten or twelve students, so that the assessment through a clinic in principle would be feasible (García-Añón, 2016), — or advisable — only for limited groups, such as those of any optional course.

Final Observations

With enough commitment by the teachers that drive it and by the institutions that house it, any legal clinic experience has the potential to turn into an academic success in many of our faculties. The clinical methodology proves to be suitable for developing important values and basic legal skills. Responsibility, team work and networking, leadership capacity, interdisciplinarity or the instruments to identify ethical conflicts are some of these skills that the clinics promote and that the leading law firms are requesting.

The transfer of knowledge from the university to society finds a privileged space within the clinics. In particular, the use of the strategic litigation techniques and concepts in human rights may make it possible for the collaborative work of students and teachers to not only produce great educational results but also considerable contributions in terms of safeguarding human rights. This, today, seems to be more needed than ever.

References

Aristóteles (2014). *Ética a Nicómaco*. Madrid: Alianza.

Bain, K. (2005). *El que fan els millors professors universitaris*. Valencia: Publicacions de la Universitat de València.

Blázquez Martín, D. (2006). Apuntes acerca de la educación jurídica clínica. *Universitas, Revista de Filosofía, Derecho y Política, 3*. 43-60.

Bloch, F. ed. (2013). *El movimiento global de clínicas jurídicas*. Valencia: Tirant lo Blanch.

Ferrajoli, L. (1999). *Derechos y garantías. La ley del más débil*. Madrid: Trotta.

Finch, E. & Fafinski, S. (2015, 5th. ed.), *Legal Skills* Oxford: Oxford UP.

García-Añón, J. ed. (2013), *Transformaciones en la docencia y el aprendizaje del derecho*. Valencia: Universitat de València.

— (2014). La integración de la educación jurídica clínica en el proceso formativo de los juristas. *REDU, Revista de Docencia Universitaria, 12* (3), 153-175.

— (2016). How do we assess in Clinical Legal Education? A "reflection" about reflective learning. *International Journal of Clinical Legal Education, 23*, 48-65.

García-Añón, J. *et al* (2008). Diseño de materiales para el aprendizaje de habilidades jurídicas fundamentales. *@atic revista d´innovació educativa,*

1, 37-44.

García-Pascual, C. coord. (2013). *El buen jurista. Deontología del derecho*. Valencia: Tirant lo Blanch.

García-Saez, J. A. & Vañó-Vicedo, R. eds. (2015). *Educar la mirada. Documentales para una enseñanza crítica de los derechos humanos*. Valencia: Tirant lo Blanch, Valencia, 2015

Gascón-Cuenca, A., Ghitti, C. & Malzani, F. (2018). Acknowledging the relevance of empathy in Clinical Legal Education. Some proposals from the experience of the University of Brescia (IT) and Valencia (ESP). *International Journal of Clinical Legal Education, 25* (2), 218-247.

González Morales, F. (2003). *El trabajo clínico en materia de derechos humanos e interés público en América Latina*. Bilbao: Universidad de Deusto.

Kennedy, D. (2014). *La enseñanza del derecho como forma de acción política*. Buenos Aires: Siglo XXI.

Mestre i Mestre, R. coord. (2018). *Guía práctica para la enseñanza del derecho a través de clínicas jurídicas*. Valencia: Tirant lo Blanch.

Molina Saldarriaga, C. A. (2008). Fundamentos teóricos y metodológicos del método clínico de enseñanza del Derecho. *Revista de la Facultad de Derecho y Ciencias Políticas, 38*, 187-213.

Torres Villarreal, M. L. *et al* eds. *El interés público en América Latina: reflexiones desde la educación legal clínica y el trabajo ProBono*. Bogotá: Universidad del Rosario.

Villarreal, M & Courtis, C. coords. (2007). *Enseñanza clínica del derecho. Una alternativa a los métodos tradicionales de formación de abogados*. México: CLIP/ITAM.

Witker, J. (2007). La enseñanza clínica como recurso de aprendizaje jurídico. *Academia. Revista sobre la enseñanza del derecho, 10*, 181-207.

Silvia Mondino

The community Lawyering Clinic in Prison

Introduction

Based on an experience of community lawyering clinic in prison, the paper highlightes characteristics and complexities related to the interaction among the clinic and the prisoner community. This work is done with the intention of demonstrating how the activities developed in the community lawyering clinic in prison, from a pedagogical perspective, represents the experimentation of a socio-constructivist approach to learning. This learning environment is paramount in the development of the project, with low-structured situations in which students, benefiting from their work with their peers, can experience new challenges that stimulate their cognitive resources. Moreover, the paper stresses out that a specific attention to the learning method also allows to define in a more precise way useful activities to ensure – in line with what was suggested by the rebellious lawyers – the empowerment of prisoners in exercising their own rights and to develop original paths of research.

Learning at the Boundary: Clinicians in Prison

The security policies that have been a feature of almost all the western countries in recent years have led to the implementation of the imprisonment phenomenon (Wacquant, 2000; Garland, 2004).

To guarantee security, post-modern controls have tended to exclude from collective spaces, understood in various ways, "non-conformist" behaviors (Ewick, 1988).

As it is well known, prison has mainly become a place to close away and contain the fears of the public, isolating especially those categories of people who, for one reason or another, are already victims of social marginalisation, and thus deepening ethnic and social inequalities.

In this scenario, prison contributes to impose a social categorisation on individuals, by strengthening (Tajfel, 1981), the distinction between who is ingroup – outside of prison – and who is outgroup – who is in prison.

Prison is perceived from the outside – but also from the inside – in an extremely conflictual manner, even because of the security policies mentioned above, tends to become a "border zone" or "frontier" area. This is so from various points of view.

On one hand, inside prison there is an extremely complex world, with its own rules and statutes. On the other hand, anyone who comes into contact with this world – such as the clinical students – has the impression of going beyond "the borders of what is known".

Prison is also a frontier area for a legal clinic, both from the teaching and learning perspective, since the type of issues that arise are often on the borderline between one discipline and another. Despite their representation, it turns out that detainees face every day the difficulties caused by deprivation of liberty: amongst the many, enjoyment of the right to health, the right to work, with questions connected with family rights or with problems associated with release and not only those associated to penitentiary law and to penal execution (Blengino, 2018b).

Lastly, it is frontier territory because all the social players involved, detainees and operators, appear to require continually that their positions are defined, to one side or the other of an invisible border, which might be simplified into "either the side of the guards or that of the guarded".

In western Europe there are various legal clinics dealing with prison[1].

As far as Italy is concerned, in terms of prison matters, there are four legal clinics: in Florence, Turin, Perugia and Rome.

This interest in the prisons has been intensified because of structural dysfunction in the Italian prison system, as demonstrated by the sentence of the European Court of Human Rights, which found Italy in breach of art. 3

---

[1] As reconstructed by Blengino (2015, p. 163) the longest standing clinical program is that of the Legal Clinic in Bremen, since 1977, jointly by the University of Bremen and the Verein für Rechtshilfe im Justizvollzug des Landes Bremen e.V. There have been two interesting experiences in this field also in Spain. The first was the Clinica Derecho y Carcel set up by the Spanish University of Rovira y Virgili, since 2002 to 2005. The second, which has now become established, is the Clìnica penitenciaria y de centros de internamiento of the University of Valencia, since 2006.

of the European Convention on Human Rights (ECHR)[2], on account of the inhuman and degrading conditions the prisoners are kept in.

The prevalent clinical model is that of *legal aid*, which is carried out, in most cases, through a special desk inside the prison, run together with NGOs.

In the legal clinic Prison and Rights I in Turin[3] the early years we decided to adopt by the *street law* clinical method.

The reason for this decision may be ascribed to the fact that often Italian students who follow degree courses in law do not all become lawyers, but might become legal operators in other fields – for istance, policemen, notaries, judges. Moreover, not necessarily questions affecting the daily lives of prisoners can be resolved through a lawyer[4].

Over time, though, the clinical activities, which had didactic aims as well as the hope of working *for* the prisoners, changed considerably: as a result of the various feedback both from the students and from the prisoners themselves, it took on the structure of a *community lawyering clinic*, which works *with* the prisoners.

The experimentation that was carried out in the correctional facility in Turin took place over two activities. One was the rethinking of the interview area inside the prison in Turin, carried out with students of law, architecture and prisoners and followed by the actual reconstruction of the area itself (Blengino, 2018a). The other activity was focused on socio-employment reintegration, carried out initially from a desk in prison. The latter was jointly run by free students of law and inmates who study law as well, who were to follow the realisation of an accompanied pathway on release.

When I define our legal clinic as a *community lawyering clinic* I integrate it into a bigger group of clinical faculty characterized by widely varying types of work.

It shares with the other *community lawyering clinics* the three core principles (Tokarz et oth., 2008: pp. 363). First, it aims "to identify and address client community issues": the clinic in Turin is focused on inmates as a community, not as singular clients. Secondly, it is "focused on empowering communities, promoting economic and social justice and fostering system change": the clinic would like to remove the obstacles that prevent the exercizes of human rights of inmates. Finally, "the work [...] involves collabo-

---

2 https://www.giustizia.it/giustizia/it/mg_1_20_1.wpfacetNode_1=1_2(2013)&facetNode_2=0_8_1_85&previsiousPage=mg_1_20&contentId=SDU810042

3 This paper refers and will discuss on the activities of legal clinic Prison and Rights 1of the University of Turin, in which I have worked for some years. It is one of the five legal clinics operating in the Department of Law of the University of Turin.

4 For a precise explanation on this point refer to Blengino 2018a.

rative and frequently interdisciplinary, practice": the clinic deals with criminologists, social workers, architects.

Amongst the different form, our legal clinic is based on "co- production"
(Blumenberg, 1998; Cahn, 2000) focusing on a search of "synergies between
the client community and the lawyer, such that the outcome is truly a product of their joint efforts" (Tokarzs et oth., 2008: pp. 366).

3. Prison: a Place or a Community?

Understanding the complexity of the juridical field of prisons (Sarzotti,
2010) is fundamental to being able to analyse how enjoyment of prisoners'
rights may differ from one prison structure to another.

The number of prisoners in Italy was 58,223 on 30 March 2018[5], of whom
19,811[6] were foreigners. However, these are just one of the categories of players involved in the so-called juridical field of prisons, which, nevertheless,
includes many other subjects, such as the officials of the pedagogical juridical
professionals, psychologists, the Department of Prison Administration, the
Regional Supervisor of Prison Administration, the cultural mediators, the
prison officers, the Prison Warden, the administrative staff, the Office for
Non-Custodial Sentencing, the Ombudsman for the rights of inmates, the
prison volunteers, the University, doctors, lawyers, judges, ministers of faith.

The concept of field (Bourdieu, 1986) is especially useful because it
affords a good explanation of how life in prison is regulated not only by
written rules[7], but also by unwritten rules that are negotiated between the
various players.

This specification proves to be indispensable: our legal clinic has decided
to work with "a community within the community".

The choice of the *community of prisoners* as beneficiary – and participant
in the case of the community lawyering clinic – proves to be based theoret-
ically on the reflections of a number of authors (including, amongst them,
Clemmer, 1940 and Sykes, 1958), who have pointed out how a stay in prison
creates and fosters consolidation of a group, subject in a different way from
the so-called prisonization process.

---

5 Despite to the official capacity of the institutions to host 50,613 persons.

6 Source: Ministry of Justice https://www.giustizia.it/giustizia/it/mg_1_14_1.page;jsessio-
nid=nEccqWoJK9bxCSwvCTyZS-Oe?contentId=SST107117&previsiousPage=mg_1_14
(last access 22 April 2018).

7 Such as the Italian Penitentiary Law n. 354/1975 – recently updated by Legislative
Decrees n. 123/2018 and 124/2018 – and Presidential Decree n. 230/1990.

The set of prisoners inside a prison structure may effectively be considered a group since it represents a dynamic whole with its own characteristics which differ from those of its sub-groups and individual members (Lewin 1951, pp. 253).

In the case of the inmates, the macroscopic element of unification is "interdependence of destiny" (Lewin 1951), which is a condition that may transform any social aggregate, if the environmental circumstances create the sensation of sharing a common destiny[8].

Inmates, being people presenting similar motivations, deprivations or frustrations, are prone to interact with each other (Sherif 1967, pp. 98-99). Inside a prison, the interaction lasts over time, so relationships are likely to become stable on various levels, in relation to the individuals involved and to external factors. In this way, a group structure is set up, where individuals are bonded between each other by relationships of status and roles, within which rules and shared values find room. In effect, inmates show a tendency to get organised, guaranteeing higher status, and therefore power of initiative, for some of them and interacting on the basis of prison codes and sub-cultures (Hester and Eglin, 1992).

Community Lawyering

One of the central aspects that characterize the community lawyering clinic is the relationship sets between students and members of the community with whom the clinic is carried on.

In common with the other examples of community lawyering clinics, the building of trust relationships with the community is extremely difficult. In fact, in addition to what may be termed as the ordinary complexity, it must be taken into account the peculiarities related to the interaction with people who live in a situation of deprived liberty. Students may be used as vehicles of communication with the outside world or may be perceived as subjects to be educated to the prison universe, lacking any specific competence and therefore unreliable. In the prison context, the power dynamics are taken to the extreme and this presupposes the need for specific preparation of the students for the environment, but also negotiation with the prisoners on how the clinic may work together with them.

What happens, from a social viewpoint is that the *prisoners community* and the students should create a new community, distinct from the previous one,

---

8 That is what happened, for example, in 1973 in Stockholm, when bank robbers took four bank clerks hostage for five days: a group atmosphere was created which led to solidarity between the parties (Stockholn Syndrome).

which works together to guarantee enjoyment of rights for the prisoners. In reality, on a practical level, the *prisoners community* sees itself as the group that is preparing itself to take in *new members*. One of the difficulties is then linked to the fact that, even in the entrance stage, these newcomers propose a change to the interactions already established in the group: passing from inter-dependence of destiny to interdependence of purpose (Lewin, 1951), where the purpose of the group determines a bond between the individuals, so that the results of the actions of each member has implications on the others. The students, then, with the activity of the clinic, propose a new type of community.

The group of clinical students thus finds itself facing a period of *apprenticeship* and observation by the prisoners, who see themselves as *senior members* of the group. This is why it is useful to review some of the playing for time techniques suggested by Moreland and Levine (1989). First of all, it is necessary to play the part of a new member. The newcomers have to play *anxious and cautious* and leave room and credibility to the old timers. Also, it is a good idea to look for a trusted contact, in other words an old timer who helps novices to become full members of the group. In the specific case of our legal clinic one of the strategies is to exploit the double role of one of the teachers, who also deals with prisoners who are studying at university, who is already known and accepted by the group of inmates, making her take on the role of *trusted contact*.

In addition to this situation there is the fact that the clinical students, as mentioned, while they are aspiring members, provide innovations, even before belonging to the group, and try to propose cooperation with the community for a specific purpose. This situation, of *anticipatory settling in* (Levine and Moreland, 1985) might have consequences in the life of the group -even when the clinic is not on the spot- upsetting some of the old timers.

A further reason for diffidence among the prisoners is often the presumption of accomplished knowledge of the rules that regulate their condition and the consequent indifference to cooperation intended to implement enjoyment of their rights.

In this respect, it is necessary, for negotiating one's role and then for reaching the consequent goal of promoting social changes and effective access to justice, to start by listening to the needs of the inmates (Denckla and Diller, 2000, p. 19).

The theoretical presupposition, shared by the *rebellious lawyers*, from which we started out, is the importance that has to be given to the "third dimension practice of law" (White, 1988, pp. 760-762). Often people in situations of vulnerability or victims of injustice are not at ease, but they do not understand who or what to blame and struggle to answer the lawyer who asks what problem they are suffering from. In this respect, giving value to the *third dimension* implies the need for "translating felt experience into understandings and actions that increase their power" (White, 1988, p. 760).

The tendency towards infantilization of the inmates by the whole institution leads then to another specific barrier in prison, namely the extreme difficulty of the prisoners in behaving as an active part of the clinical process.

However, encouraging their participation, especially when they are subjects with long sentences, also proves to be a tool for ensuring subsequent effective re-socialization, without completely betraying the goals that the 1975 reform law set itself.

Benefits of Community Lawyering for Clinical Legal Education and Client Communities

Community lawyering as a law learning laboratory in action

Our legal clinic is based on a socio-constructivist educational approach: interest focus on the individual cognitive actions, but above all on the cognitive relationships that occur between the subjects and the socio-cultural context they are implicated in.

Under this approach, which differs significantly from that of the cognitivist framework – which applies a hierarchical, progressive structure to learning (Gagnè, 1962) – the learning environment is placed in the forefront, with lowly structured situations where the student can engage with his/her colleagues and experiment on problems that stimulate his/her cognitive resources.

During their activities in the community lawyering clinic, students find themselves constantly facing *situations-problem*. This concept is interpreted as a circumstance having three characteristics (Fabre, 1999). First of all it must be such as to push them to develop knowledge and skills that acquire significance because they allow them to experiment in a certain field; it must give support to the students' initiative and must be linked to their own practices of current life.

During the first encounter with the situation-problem – which is normally more complex and different from what they are accustomed to imagining – the risk is that the students will step back and the members of the prisoner community will play an extremely demanding role towards them, without thinking of giving any specific support at all to the solution.

The clinical teacher's task in this circumstance is similar to that of a film director, who knows and can direct all the actors, but leaves them free to experiment.

In a moment of impasse between prisoners and students in the community lawyering clinic in prison, it is good for the teacher to use a route of "a learning spiral" (Bruner, 1960, p. 33). This means that, faced by a complex situation, such as that of the residence for prisoners and ex-prisoners is during the activity relating to the accompanied process of release of prisoners, activities of structured learning are pursued, such as examination of regulatory texts and meeting with an executive of the prison officers, leading to increased difficulty of tasks[9].

In our opinion, success of the clinical activity depends largely also on the success of the community lawyering clinic as a mode of learning, taking place in horizontal forms between students and between students and prisoners (cooperative learning). The conditions for a positive outcome of this learning are that the goal is perceived as vital, that it is shared by all members of the group and that it is an invitation to the challenge (Chiosso, 2018). Another central aspect is the *climate*, namely that the relationships between the people do not create closed or defensive attitudes. This last aspect has to be monitored constantly, to avoid *weighing down* the students excessively in the prison environment, since they are normally less able to evade the abusive attitudes sometimes adopted by prisoners, and help them achieve contact with the prisoners that shows respect for the roles of each of them. This is why our legal clinic provides a dedicated coaching on communication and proxemics technique managed by criminologist to whom is given fortnightly reports on the meetings in prison, which were then discussed in class with the students.

Through these reports – for which the questions are set by the teachers – the students also learn how to listen to and assess the third dimension practice of law, which will help them during their professional activity in understanding how to identify the legal question underlying the claims of their clients.

Community lawyering as fertile ground for research

One of the more interesting aspects – from a certain point of view unexpected – generated by the community lawyering clinic in prison is the emergence of new avenues of research[10], since the students were oriented not only towards problem solving, but also towards problem finding, that is, discovering issues emerging gradually as the situation unfolds.

---

9 Initially the students are concentrated on what concerns the documents and methods for declaring residence in the registry office, then they assess the relationships between the registry office and Public Authorities and, lastly, the specific agreements between prisons and registry offices regarding the matter of residence.

10 Such as issues linked to the concrete consequences of failure of the prisoner or ex-pri-

The working approach we teach to the students, which has led to the development of several action research cases in prison, is that of the reflective professional (Schön, 1983). Assuming the idea that problems do not show up already fixed, the professional has to make a preliminary analysis before formulating a consistent response. In this sense, the plan of action is structured in five steps: defining the situation as an issue, starting exploratory experimentation, "testing the move", testing the "hypothesis", testing the situation (Schön, 1983, p. 145-147). In this view, knowledge and action are inseparably linked, so the professionals take on the role of "investigators encountering a problematic situation whose reality they have to construct" (Schön, 1983, p. 182). This method of proceeding connects back very clearly to the principles of action research, on the basis of which, by using a circular set up, cause and action act in a synergistic and reciprocal form. The clinical students therefore find themselves going beyond the traditional horizons of pure research and carrying out research into the reality in which they are acting, also perceiving the transformational nature of the process of knowledge and the relationship between researcher and group with and on the research being carried out.

Community lawyering as instrument to promote access to rights.

The community lawyering clinic is extremely helpful for the prisoners, because they feel responsibilized in a context in which that almost never happens. At the same time, they have a door on to the outside and on to society and that makes them less isolated.

The community lawyering clinic in prison develops a type of *organizational learning* in favor of the prisoner community. This is structured in three successive stages: transformation of the information into knowledge, transformation of the knowledge into know how and transformation of the know how into operational behavior (Quaglino, 1999, p. 222-223). The various clinical moments are spelled out by group encounters involving students and prisoners. Initially students and prisoners try to formulate the legal question together and identify possible limits to its resolution (at this point the above mentioned period of impasse normally sets in). After this the students bring material on rules and jurisprudence discussing it with the prisoners. Lastly they try together to define how this law may be operationally put into action.

In this manner they try to "favor the growth of experiential and cultural cognitive resources which, with its effective potential, enables survival and development of organisations" (Chiosso, 2018, p. 60).

By working with the clinical students, the prisoners acquires knowledge and competence, to be understood as the capacity for resolving not just a

---

soner to register with the registry office.

101

complex solution, but all the situations comparable with the first one every time they arise.

The latent goal of the community lawyering clinic might become that of building up critical consciences – and not just instrumental abilities – that can lead the prisoners to emancipation from their condition of weakness.

This end is what was identified by Schwartz in his prospect of *lifelong learning*. According to this author, what is, by the way, central to the strategy in this sense – and this is what happens in the community lawyering clinic- is the real concreteness of the educational experiences and the personal participation as well as the insertion of education into the environment.

Conclusions

The activities developed in the community lawyering clinic in prison, starting from a pedagogic perspective, are nothing other than the experimentation of a socio-constructivist learning approach, where the learning environment is placed in the foreground and has to be investigated and analysed by the teacher in relation to the possible inter- and intra-group dynamics.

At the same time, concentrating on the pedagogic instruments regarding learning, within the community lawyering clinic, makes it possible to define more precisely the ways and the activities that help to guarantee, in line with what is suggested by the rebellious lawyers, the empowerment of prisoners, with reference to the rights they may exercise. As well as developing, at the same time, new paths for research.

References

Blengino, C., (2015), Formare il giurista oltre il senso comune penale. Il ruolo della clinical legal education in carcere, in C. Blengino (ed.), *Stranieri e sicurezza. Il volto oscuro dello stato di diritto*, Napoli: ESI pp. 151-183.

Blengino, C., (2018a), Interdisciplinarity and clinical legal education: how synergies can improve access to rights in prison, in *International Journal of Clinical Legal Education*, Northumbria University, 25, 1, pp. 210 – 239.

Blengino, C., (2018b), Formazione dal basso, approccio interdisciplinare, impegno civile: fondamenti teorici dell'esperienza clinica legale con detenuti e vittime di tratta, in Maestroni A., Brambilla P., Carrer M.(eds.), *Teorie e pratiche nelle cliniche legali*, Torino: Giappichelli.

Blumenberg A. et al., (1998), A Co-Production Model of Code Enforcement and Nuisance Studies, in *Crime prevention studies*, pp. 261- 262.

Bourdieu, P., (1986), La force du droit: élément pur une sociologie du droit in *Actes de la recherche en Sciences Sociales*, 64, pp. 3-19.

Brooks, S. L. & Lopez, R., (2015), Designing a Clinic Model for a Restorative Community Justice Partnership (October 3, 2015). 48 *Wash. U. J. L. & Pol'y 139* (2015). Available at SSRN: https://ssrn.com/abstract=2669003

Bruner, J. S., (1960), *The Process of Education*. MA: Harvard University Press; it. transl. *Il processo educativo. Dopo Dewey*, Roma: Armando, 1966.

Cahn, E., (2000), Co-Producing Justice: The New Imperative, in *5 D.C.L. Rev.* 105.

Chiosso, G., (2018), *Studiare pedagogia. Introduzione ai significati dell'educazione*, Milano: Mondadori Università.

Clemmer, D., (1940), *The prison community*, Boston: The Christopher Publishing Co.

Denckla, D. & Diller, M., (2000), Community Lawyering: Theory and Practice, *Other Publications*. Book 1. http://ir.lawnet.fordham.edu/stein_other/1.

Diamond, M. R., (2015), Community Lawyering: Introductory Thoughts on Theory and Practice. *Georgetown Law Faculty Publications and Other Works*. 1648. https://scholarship.law.george-town.edu/facpub/164

Ewick, P., (1988), Punishment, Power, and Justice, in Garth, B. G, Sarat, A. (ed.), *Justice and power in sociolegal studies*, Evanston: Northwestern University Press, pp. 36-54.

Fabre, M., (1999), *Situations- problèmes et savoir scolaire*, Paris: PUF.

Gagne, R. M., (1962), Military training and principles of learning. *American Psychologist*, 17, 263-276.

Garland, D., (2001), *The Culture of Control*, :The University of Chicago Press.

Hester, S. & Eglin P., (1992), *A sociology of Crime*, New York: Routledge.

Imai, S.,(2002), A Counter-pedagogy for Social Justice: Core Skills for Community Lawyering, *Clinical Law Review* 9.1, pp. 195-227

Levine, J.M. & Moreland, R.L., (1985), Innovation and socialization in small groups, in Moscovici S., Mugny G. & Van Avermaet E. (eds.), *Perspectives on minority influence*, Cambridge: Cambridge University Press.

Levine, J.M. & Moreland, R.L., (1990), Progress in small group research, in *Annual Review of Psychology*, 41, pp. 585-634.

Lewin, K., (1951), *Field theory in social science*, New York: Harper & Row.

Loewy, K. L., (2000), Lawyering for Social Change, *27 Fordham Urb. L.J.* 1869. Available at: https://ir.lawnet.fordham.edu/ulj/vol27/iss6/4

Lopez, G.P., (1992), *Rebellious Lawyering: One Chicano's Vision of Progressive Law Practice*, University of Texas: Westview Press.

Mondino, S., (2015), Lo straniero come destinatario delle ordinanze urbane in materia di incolumità pubblica e sicurezza urbana, in C. Blengino (ed.), *Stranieri e sicurezza. Il volto oscuro dello stato di diritto*, Napoli: ESI pp. 81-112.

Quaglino, G. P., (1999), *Scritti di formazione, 1978-1998*, Milano: Angeli.

Sarzotti, C., (2010), Il campo giuridico penitenziario. Appunti per una ricostruzione. In E. Santoro (ed), *Diritto come questione sociale*, Torino: Giappichelli.

Schön, D., (1983), *The Reflective Practitioner: How Professionals Think In Action,* Basic Books, New York.

Schwartz, B., (1995), *Modernizzare senza escludere*, Roma: Anicia.

Sherif, M., (1967), *Social interaction, process and products*, Chicago, Ill.: Aldine publishing Company.

Sykes, G., (1958), *The Society of Captives: A Study of a Maximum Security Prison, The British Journal of Delinquency* Vol. 9, 4 (April, 1959), pp. 307-309.

Tajfel, H., (1981), *Human groups and social categories. Studies in social psychology*, Cambridge: Cambridge University Press..

Tokarz K., Cook N.L., Brooks S., and Bratton Blom B. (2008) Conversations on "Community. Lawyering": The Newest (Oldest) Wave in Clinical Legal Education, in *28 Wash. U. J.L. & Policy*, pp. 359- 382

Wacquant, L., (2000), *Parola d'ordine tolleranza zero. La trasformazione dello stato penale nella società neoliberale*, Milano: Feltrinelli.

White, L., (1988), To Learn and to Teach: Lessons from Dreifontein on Lawyering and Power, *Wis. L. Rev*, 699, pp.760-766.

CLAUDIO SARZOTTI

Carceral Tours and Penal Tourism:
a didactic tool for the understanding of the total institution

Introduction

For some years, as part of my courses in the Department of Law at the University of Turin, I have introduced the didactic practice of making my students visit prisons currently in operation and the *Museum of prison memory* in Saluzzo (C. Sarzotti, 2013). This methodology is not totally unknown in Italy[1], but no reflection has ever been made on it regarding the effects it has produced, either in terms of didactic goals achieved or on how the prison system perceived it and contributed to organising it.

The issue of external persons visiting total institutions is a classic issue of the sociological sector studying them. Erving Goffman (1961) devoted a whole chapter of *Asylums* to the so-called "institutional ceremonies", using this expression to designate those institutionalised practices through which the staff and the inmates get closer to one another, in such a way that they obtain an image of one another that is in some way favourable, sufficiently to identify mutually. These ceremonies have the function to abandon for a short period the formalities and the rigid hierarchy characterising the relationships between staff and inmates, "relaxing" the relations between the

---

1 To my knowledge, at least as far as teaching in departments of Law is concerned, visits to or cooperation with prisons is carried out at the Universities of Florence, Roma Tre and Bologna. In particular, Prof. Renzo Orlandi organised a study tour with a visit to the prison in Turin and to the *Museum of prison memory,* within his course of criminal procedure at the University of Bologna.

individuals who are obliged to cohabit forcibly within the total institution. These institutional ceremonies also include the visits of external persons[2]. They are often real and proper institutional "set ups", prepared for visitors to respond to a double goal. First, looking inwards, they aim to convince both the inmates and the staff that the total institution is not a world in itself, but that it has a place within a wider social and institutional structure. Then the inmates and the staff have a legitimate role to play in the free world, even though that legitimacy is paradoxically strictly linked to that very condition of social separateness and subordination. Secondly, looking outwards, these ceremonies are aimed at visitors for the purpose of offering them an image of the organisation, intended to dissipate the vague terror they feel towards enforced institutions (E. Goffman, 1961, 129). The total institution tries on these occasions to show its best face and, especially, tries to reaffirm in the eyes of the visitors its ability to pursue the institutional mission that society has entrusted it with.

Analysing the ways in which these events are put together then becomes very interesting for understanding how the total institution conceives of itself in relation to the outside world. Through analysis of how the total institution builds up its own self-representation the picture also emerges of the elements that it considers acceptable and presentable to the public opinion. From this point of view, Goffman (1961, 130) underlines how the façade that the institution habitually shows is probably the new, modern part, which will change every time that modernisations and additions are made. Often the representation will not concentrate on essential aspects of the institutional mission, but on apparently marginal details, such as technologically advanced equipment or inmates who display some special talent in working or artistic activities. These are elements that permit a reassuring image of the performance of the institution and, especially, show that the inmate's personality is respected, while they are often shown carrying out activities that put their time to good use. This is evidently a strategy of *excusatio non petita*[3], which casts light in an indirect manner on the more critical elements of the total institution: the processes of infantilization the inmates are subjected to and the organisational dysfunctions very often displayed by the total institutions on account of lack of investments and poor outside control

---

2 Amongst the institutional ceremonies, Goffman quotes the periodicals that are produced inside the total institutions with the cooperation of the inmates, the annual parties (often held at Christmas time) where the inmates can meet their relatives and the theatrical shows, as well as sporting events involving the inmates in leading roles and which are often also open to the outside public.

3 N.d. A. The latin aphorism *Excusatio non petita accusatio manifesta* is used to mean that a not required excuse is an evident self-accusation.

over the efficiency of the services provided.

Unlike what has happened in Italy, in the anglo-saxon context the sociology of prison life has made an extensive study of the phenomenon of visits to prison institutions (or kindred total institutions), whether as instruments of ethnographic research or as didactic instruments for university students. In this regard, the effects have also been analysed with regard to the didactic visits to prison museums. This greater attention is explicable not only because of the greater diffusion of these didactic and research practices, but also because of the greater sophistication of the organisational level of the prison systems in that context, which have produced genuine formally organised strategies to regulate the "spectacles" put on by the prison institutes during visits by outside subjects.

In countries like Canada and the United States, the university teaching programmes on criminal justice, both for courses in law degrees and those of a socio-anthropological nature, very often include visits to prisons and museums dealing with that subject. These activities are very appreciated by the students and promoted by the university programs, which highlight these tours in their on-line prospectuses. The tours are organised jointly between the university structures and prison administrations, following extremely strict, detailed guidelines. When the students enter the prison structure, they undergo "training", where they are warned of the dangers they may encounter and the procedures they have to follow. They are usually given instructions to stay with their guide, to walk along the walls of the corridors when they move around from one section to another and to avoid any contact with the prisoners, including exchange of greetings, conversations or even direct eye contact (T. Arford, 2017).

The organisational strategies have been formalised to such an extent by the prison administrations that it was possible to analyse their guidelines[4]. Many elements emerging from these research projects are also found in the Italian situation, with the only, far from irrelevant, difference that the "set up" strategies produced by the prison administration are almost entirely non-formalized and therefore linked to choices of the individual managements of the prisons involved. The more informal manner in which these visits are managed make them even more interesting from the point of view of sociological research into prison life, since aspects emerge more freely both on the prison operators' professional culture and the inmates' sub-culture. This essay proposes to analyse, in a preliminary stage of more structured empirical research, the experience of the prison visits the Author has experimented with during his didactic and research activities. I will try, first

---

4 Particularly regarding the state of Canada which has given rise to debate as to the legitimacy and usefulness of such visits (J. Piché, K. Walby, 2010; H. Thurston, 2017, 6).

of all, to show the specifics of the Italian case and then make some considerations on what impact these visits had on the students, from the point of view of didactic goals, and on what precautions should be taken, in order to reach the didactic ends of bringing under discussion the stereotypes that exist in the popular culture with regard to prison. In this last part, I will also attempt to take a reasoned stance towards the dilemma, which is also of an ethical nature, of whether it is legitimate and useful to continue making these visits.

The Turin experience in relation to the international literature

The observed data which will be taken into consideration in this research refer to both visits to prisons still in activity at the time of the visit, and to a museum site open in the ex-prison called the *Castiglia di Saluzzo* since 2014[5]. In the former connection, I will take into consideration both the visits regularly made by my students over the course of the last five years and the ones made as part of the *Summer School* organised by the University of Turin and the NGO Antigone[6] since September 2017[7]. My reflection will also benefit from my consolidated experience as observer for the Antigone's Observatory on Prison Conditions in Italy. In the latter connection, I will examine, on the other hand, the visits to the *Museum of prison memory* made by myself with my students of Law, as from the Museum's inauguration. This evidently represents a limited number of visits, with regard to which the observed data are still at an experimental level. The considerations that will be put forward therefore make no presumptions to be considered representative of the Italian situation, but simply aim to lay the basis for wider and more methodologically accurate empirical research. Considering the vast difference between the two locations visited, one a working prison and the other a prison museum, the considerations put forward will stay separated and will be presented in the order just shown.

5 To gain an idea of the content of the Museum of prison memory, as well as the essay by C. Sarzotti (2013), please make a visit to the website www.museodellamemoriacarceraria.it

6 Antigone is an Italian cultural and political NGO that was born in the late eighties, devoted to promote rights and guarantees in the penal system. It is supported by magistrates, workers in the penitentiary system, lawyers, researchers, parliamentarians, teachers and ordinary citizens interested in criminal justice (www.antigone.it)..

7 We are referring to the *Summer Shool on Deprivation of Fundamental Liberty and,* managed since 2017 by the Departement of Law. It is a training course, addressing jurists and students in law, focused on how to guarantee rights for persons deprived of personal liberty (thus not only detained due to criminal convictions) even before international courts (eg CEDU).

Acceptance of the prison visit

A first element to be taken into consideration is how the prison adminis-tration looks on the visit to the institute and interferes in the manner in which it is carried out. In the anglo-saxon literature it has been noted that the limi-tations almost always placed by the prison administration "suggest that tours are always viewed as a risk to prison order (security and discipline)" (Piché, Walby, 2010, 572). In the meantime, the objective the prison administration usually sets itself is that, "to demonstrate our openness and integrity by pro-moting public understanding of the objectives and operations of Springhill Institution through official and public visit" (*ivi*, 571). Thus the total institu-tion has to balance its own interest to show that it is open to the outside, con-futing the stereotype of the prison that isolates itself from the outside world, with the risk that the outside visitor may observe a reality that is often very different from that which the institutional mission would require.

In the visits analysed in this research, this double objective, which is often difficult to reconcile, is further emphasised in the case of the visits of the NGO Antigone for the *Observatory on Prison Conditions in Italy*. This observatory, even though it does not hold real powers of inspection in relation to the Italian prison administration, is intended to publish a report to bring out the critical points of the prison administration with regard to its ability to guarantee the rights laid down by the regulations, both for detained persons (first and foremost) and for persons who work there (in an indirect way)[8]. On the other hand though, facing students' request to enter the pris-ons, the attitude of the prison administration becomes much more relaxed and almost pleased, inasmuch as the university institution is looked on as an institution that can give prestige. The fact that cultured individuals belong-ing to social classes that are in any case privileged, as are lecturers (above all) and students (generally), should devote their time to approach the world of prisons is perceived as a symptom of non-total marginality of this institu-ition. In the case of law professors and students – i.e. jurists whether already affirmed or in course of instruction –, there is the additional factor that many prison staff, such as wardens, are graduates in Law, who look up to and have a certain inferiority complex towards university law teachers.

This attitude emerges at least in two circumstances. Very often the visits start and spend rather a long time in the administration offices of the manage-ment, before reaching the detention areas. In particular, the place for initial

---

8 The report has reached its fourteenth edition, most of them published in the maga-zine *Antigone. Four-monthly criticism of the penal and prison system*, and which since two years ago is only available on-line (see the latest edition in http://www.antigone.it/ quattordicesimo-rapporto-sulle-condizioni-di-detenzione/).

reception of visitors is represented by the prison director's office, which is normally distinguishable from all the others by the elegance of the furnishing and its spaciousness. But even when it is not the warden who directly accompanies the visitors, the initial reception does not take place in the detention departments, but in the administration offices. It is as if those who are part of the total institution want to show anyone from outside that their work does not consist, either exclusively or mainly, in managing the detention spaces, but rather in operating within a complex organisation requiring official work and of a concept not very different from any other ministerial apparatus. I recall, during a visit made to the prison in Saluzzo with students from the *Summer School*, a long stay in the registration offices with a young prison officer who was explaining the operations of registering new inmates and the juridical questions that such apparently simple operations lead to. The young officer, who felt the need to explain exactly how that rather complex job was only possible for him on account of his degree in law, continued by praising the technology that has today done away with the old inkpads for fingerprinting, replaced by modern scanners which memorise the dactyloscopic data immediately. In the narrative of this young officer, the inhuman rituals of degradation identified by Goffman lost their de-humanising effects and took on the tone of aseptic, technologically advanced scientific procedure. The body of the detainee and the place where his/her dispossession and classification took place were thus transformed by narrative from a place of degradation into a scientific laboratory, from the body of a prisoner into the body of a patient undergoing a medical examination.

The second circumstance where this attitude emerges is related to the questions that the guides chosen by the prison administration make during the visit to the teacher accompanying the students: these questions almost always involve a request for juridical information relating to regulatory aspects of life in prison. These e questions are not intended so much to satisfy a need for information, as to demonstrate a quite sophisticated knowledge of law on the part of the person asking the actual question. A typical formulation of these questions is the following: "as you will know Professor, it seems to me that the Court of Cassation has given a verdict on this aspect, but do you understand what that verdict means in concrete terms?" In this manner, the guide shows that he/she is informed on developments, even in sophisticated aspects of law, and at the same time pleases the interlocutor by asking for clarifying advice. This is yet another demonstration of the inferiority complex towards jurists on the part of prison staff, who are afraid of being judged as second tier jurists.

Guide to the visit and related prison areas

Another element highlighted by the international literature is the fact that the administrations usually choose a guide to accompany the visitors for the whole duration of the visit. "In every Canadian federal penitentiary, there are designated staff members responsible for organizing facility tours requested by groups such as university classes and government officials. It is a responsibility of internal tour organizers to ensure the adequate preparations have been made regarding the security of tour participants as well as staff and prisoners, and to convey the desired institutional narratives and imagery to outsiders" (Piché, Walby, 2010, 572).

As mentioned, the visits to Italian prisons are much less formalised and there is therefore no evidence of measures from the Department for Prison Administration which lay down the choice and the preparation of the tour guides[9]. One sole exception was made for the tours of the contact persons of the NGO Antigone, for whom it was established that the guide must be the prison warden, or if he/she was unavailable, the commander of the prison officers or his/her delegate. This regulatory indication proves very significant inasmuch as it repeats formally a choice applied by the managements of the prisons informally, following a professional culture that is evidently very widespread: even before this measure, in effect, when it was not the warden who carried out the role of guide, the task was delegated to the commander of policemen inside the prison or, in any case his/her representative. In this manner, the components of the so-called rehabilitation area – educators, social assistants and psychologists – , are excluded from the role of guides, yet they could play an invaluable role in describing the working activities as well as those of teaching and other kinds organised for the prisoners, in order to achieve the institutional mission of the prison, as clearly described by art. 27 of the Italian Constitution. Occasionally these figures are not totally excluded from the visits, inasmuch as they are called on as "non-leading players", to illustrate individual activities carried out inside the institution: if a woodworking laboratory is visited, up pops a training official who teaches the prisoners the art of engraving on wood; if a classroom is visited, out comes the teacher, who illustrates the good results achieved by the student inmates; if the infirmary is visited, there is the nurse who explains how the

---

9 It should be pointed out that we are talking about visits of outside subjects not covered by art. 67 of the Prison Regulations, which contains a mandatory list of institutional bodies (members of Parliament, judges, regional councillors, watchdog commissioners etc.) who may visit prisons for purposes of inspection without any authorisation from the administration. For these visits the DAP issued a consolidated law, in circular no. 3651/6101 of 7 November 2013, to regulate many aspects of these visits, which, however, are for purposes and organisational dynamics very different from the visits for didactic purposes we are talking about in this essay.

institute purchases the latest drugs available, to guarantee the right to health-care for the prisoners. The choice of giving precedence to a member of the prison officers as a guide is an indication of the greater power that this sector of the prison operators possesses compared to others. The task of guiding, in effect, evidently represents a gratifying task and that reaffirms the power of the person who carries it out, also in the eyes of the visitors. The subject who "does the honours" is evidently the one who feels "the owner" of the insti-tution and is also the one who knows the details of the prison facility better than anyone else, is more adroit when moving around the areas of the var-ious sections safely and is familiar with the various activities carried on in the institution. This topographical knowledge of the facility is anything but taken for granted, especially when the institute is medium-large in dimen-sions: even when it is the warden who is guiding, he/she is almost always accompanied by an official of the prison officers in prison to show the way around. It should be pointed out, in fact, that only a few prison operators possess full knowledge and are able to move around freely inside the struc-ture. Rehabilitation operators, and sometimes even the wardens themselves, would not know how to move around without difficulty inside the institute, because they do not usually go into a large part of the sections of the facility: the former because they have no official authorisation and the latter because they do not find the time or the wish to do so[10].

Analysing the choice of spaces where the visits are carried out is also highly interesting for bringing out the features of the professional culture of the prison staff. Regarding areas that may be visited, it should first of all be underlined that it is almost never possible to visit the sections where the detained persons spend the largest part of their days in their cells. This choice is officially justified, first of all, to protect the confidentiality of the detained persons[11] and, secondly, to prevent communications becoming too informal between them and the visitors. Such communications are not expressly forbidden, but the visits are organised in such a way that the vis-itors can only enter into direct contact with a selected group of inmates in

10 It also has to be taken into consideration in this respect that in Italy, because of insuf-ficient numbers of qualified management personnel, many prisons have wardens who are so-called "on tour", or in other words wardens who have more than one prison under their management. Time to devote to inspecting the individual sections is therefore very restri-cted and this is also to prevent prisoners being able to make claims directly to the warden, without the shield of the prison officers. I have managed to observe personally prisoners who took their chance, while the warden was present as a guide for a visit of outside per-sons, to make a request for a meeting with the warden himself.

11 We will return to this argument shortly, when talking about the ethical problems relating to the visits to the total institutions.

spatial contexts other than those where they spend a large part of their day. This organisational choice enables the prison administration to achieve two results that are very important for their own communicative strategy. On one side, it allows them to select the prisoners that can show to best effect the presentable face of the total institution. On the other, it allows them to represent to the visitor a typical day for the inmate inside the total institution as being packed with working, school, sports and cultural activities, etc. On superficial examination, the ingenuous visitor may be led to think, by what he/she sees, that the inmate passes the days attending school, taking part in craft workshop activities or in real and proper employment activities, cooperating in cultural projects, such as theatre shows or painting exhibitions and stretching their legs when they feel like it, either in the gym or on the five-a-side football pitch[12]. The prisoners can enter into direct contact with the visitors in all of these contexts that are not really detention, such that they are able to appear to a superficial observer not very different from any free individual whatsoever, who may be enjoying these activities. But this is a spectacle somewhat distant from the effective reality of the total institution, when the statistics tell us that in Italy little more than 30% of the prison population perform any work inside the institutions, then only with occasional frequency and mainly on behalf of the prison administration itself, with very humble tasks, such as cleaning the corridors and giving out food in the detention sections[13]. These are also somewhat improvised spectacles and they are sometimes exposed, even by chance. An example from this point of view was the visit made to the prison in Saluzzo by a group of young participants in the *Summer School* previously mentioned. The visitors, accompanied by the warden, were taken into a laboratory for brewing beer, to find sparkling new equipment on show and cleanliness fit for a hospital ward. The warden, with the aid of an immigrant prisoner who – speaking a very good Italian and being unusually well dressed for the happening – described the production process, which involved considerable investment on the part of the outside cooperative that runs the laboratory and which had also engaged a famous master brewer. To show off the quality of the home brew produced, the visitors were also invited to a tasting, which was promptly prepared and served by the same prisoner. Goffman would have been delighted to find such a perfect incarnation of his notion of institutional

---

12   These are usually the main places and activities that are illustrated and visited on these occasions.

13   These data were provided by the same prison administration and were commented on by the observatory of the Antigone Association, cf. the latest updates http://www.antigone.it/quattordicesimo-rapporto-sulle-condizioni-di-detenzione/lavoro/ (last visited on 26/07/2018).

ceremony! But the devil always hides behind details: one of the participants on the visit, between one sip of the golden beverage and another, is moved spontaneously to ask the warden an innocent question. "How many prisoners were involved in this project?" The warden immediately switched off his smug air and started a long, tortuous and slightly cryptic speech, at the end of which it was revealed that, on account of bureaucratic questions that could not be further explained, the prisoners involved amounted to the exorbitant total of ... two! General embarrassment ensued and the "showcase" strategy was almost totally compromised[14].

Impacts on the students' perception about prison and convicted people

The anglo-saxon literature has widely discussed, and it has even been divided, over the didactic effects and of perception of the prison world on the part of students produced by the visits to the prisons (for the reconstruction of this debate cf. H.P. Smith, 2013). Empirical research has been carried out to try to measure these effects. Some research has analysed written comments requested from the students after their visit (Helfgott, 2013). Others have issued questionnaires to the students before and after the visit, to measure the effects it has produced towards the conception of punishment s (retributive, re-educational, incapacitating, etc.), the representation of the prisoner and the prison and the selectivity of criminalisation processes (Smith et al., 2009). Other research has widened the research subject to mutations also of the perception of the students towards the prison staff and their propensity to enter these professions (Stacer et al., 2016), or again to the alternative measures to prison (W.R. Calaway et al., 2016). Yet others have extended the analysis to the effects on the students from courses employing virtual prison tours and e-learning, which use film footage of juvenile prisons (K. Miner-Romanoff, 2014). Some research has set out to measure the impact of didactic programmes that go beyond simple, occasional visits, but take concrete form in genuine training courses, lasting weeks, within the prisons, through didactic methods that come close to being genuine legal clinics (L. Ridley, 2014).

As mentioned, the considerations that will be presented here are not the fruits of truly empirical research, but they represent the result of certain reflections that I have been able to develop over these years of didactic practice, through contact with the students who took part in the visits I carried out for didactic purposes, both to prisons and to the *Museum of prison memory* in Saluzzo. In this way I have managed to analyse the reactions of the

---

14 I will return to this episode when dealing with the didactic strategies to measure the effects of the visits on the students.

students, which were revealed both in informal contexts (discussions during the university lessons and those of the *summer school*), and in more formal didactic contexts, such as the written reports on subjects covered in the visit, mini-theses on conclusion of the *summer school* and oral assessment exams for student preparation. These are observations that still lack a full scientific structure, but which lay the basis for further development of the research in a context like the Italian one, where empirical research is virtually unknown.

If the effects seen on the students from the previously mentioned research are analysed, it can be seen that the students have taken up different positions on some of the fundamental didactic questions. Taking it for granted that the total institution tries to exploit these visits as part of the institutional ceremonies à la Goffman, how do the students protect themselves and/or be protected against the "construction of reality" proposed in the visits by the warden of the prison? In particular, can the students manage to take up a critical position against this? To what extent does this construction of reality put on show by the prison administration merely reaffirm the stereotypes of the prison world that circulate in the popular culture? In terms of his/her future professional aspirations, how is the student influenced by the experience, often emotively significant, of the visit? Do they change their perception of the person imprisoned and the staff working in the prison, and in what way do they change it?

Regarding these questions, the group of Italian students examined by myself present some elements common to those analysed in the international literature, while other aspects, though, differ from them.

Concerning the perception of the living conditions of the inmates inside the prison, the most widespread tendency seems to be that of considering such conditions in any case less difficult than what the students expected prior to the visit. These expectations are very much influenced by the public view of prison that is abundantly nurtured by the construction of reality by the so-called "prison movies". As is well-known, this cinema genre, which often takes on the perspective of the unjustly punished prisoner, overturns the social roles of the victim-oppressor pairing[15]. In this perspective, the film plot is often studded with abuses of power, humiliation and extremely tough conditions of prison life. This rather macabre imaginary reconstruction of prison reality existing in the popular culture may be reinforced by the concept of a retributive sentence, according to which it is completely obvious that the convicted person in prison has to suffer, in order to atone for the blame for the crime committed. The prison visit, as orchestrated by the prison administration contributes to covering up the more painful aspects of life in prison: the prisoner is not seen in the promiscuity of the cell, the eyes

---

15 For the definition of this cinema genre, cf. C. Sarzotti, G. Siniscalchi, 2013.

of the visitors are not allowed to fall on the more difficult prisoners, the ones who bear the signs of their suffering on their faces and bodies; the sense of desolation, the minor abuses of power of life in detention are totally ignored in the narrative of a daily existence devoted to work and the commitment to re-education; the places visited themselves, if exception is made for the visible presence of the bars on the windows and the disquieting metallic sound of the locks and the doors opening and closing[16], appear to be decent, sufficiently clean and not very different from any other total institution for free people. All of this produces a perception according to which the prisoner enjoys conditions of detention that are substantially acceptable, in line with what one deserves in paying the penalty and even, in certain cases, also makes use of services that gratify his/her existence in a way that is even excessive. From this perspective, one often hears the very common, typical, rather shocked expression: "But they even have television in the cell!"

As for perceptions of the person imprisoned, the effects are, on the other hand, rather distant from a reaffirmation of the stereotypes in force in the popular culture. On this aspect, I have not found in Italy any praxis described in the literature on the subject, that shows the prison administration guides emphasising the dangerousness of the prisoner or warning the visitor against interacting with them with too much trust (cf. Piché, Walby, 2010). On the contrary, it is precisely the strategy that aims to represent life in prison as that of a community that is, in the final analysis, well run and engaged in various daily activities which tends to bring out the characters of absolute normality and reliability of the imprisoned person. The typical comment of the student concerning this is: "I didn't believe they were so similar to us". This sensation grows when the visitor has the chance to exchange a few words with the prisoner or when the latter also manages to recount briefly his/her personal story that led to imprisonment. It may occur that the expression of these excerpts from personal affairs of the inmates are favoured by the guides for the visit themselves, who probably mean to use this device to show their humaneness in a good light, or demonstrate how the role of the staff goes well beyond the technical level designed to maintain security and the prison treatment of the prisoner. It is highly likely that the specific professional culture of the Italian prison staff includes an element of accentuated benevolent paternalism, deriving from the very history of the Italian prison (C. De Vito, 2009).

In any case, the chance for the persons imprisoned to bring into play storytelling of their personal affairs, which, on account of the very circumstances

---

16 These are the aspects which, according to the statements of the students who possibly possess greater sensitivity and sense of empathy, are the source of greater uneasiness for visitors who had not previously known prison.

in which this occurs, can only take on pathetic, self-absolving tones, induces a two-sided reaction in the visiting students. On the one side, the student most frequently develops a process of empathy with the inmate, which may even go as far as to perceive his/her condition as a deep injustice and to put into question the legitimacy of the prison sentence. On the other side, in a more limited number of cases, the student tends to read the affair of the inmate as confirmation of the positive effects induced on the latter by the prison. As a matter of fact, cases are not infrequent where prisoners, especially those with long spells of detention behind them, demonstrate on these occasions a surprising capacity for self-analysis of their own condition and their own existential journey, to such an extent that they appear intellectually and morally far superior to what might be expected in a person in prison[17]. In front of such accounts full of deep humanity and self-reflection, some of the students are led to believe that it was the prison that provoked the deep change and thus attribute to the sentence a cathartic function of reform of the convict[18].

The differences in the reactions to the visits highlight how essential it is, for reaching the predetermined didactic goals, to plan a stage of preparation for the visit and a subsequent stage for discussion and re-elaboration of the observations made and emotions aroused by the visit. In the specific case I am dealing with, these two stages were developed in parallel with the visit to the *Museum of prison memory* in Saluzzo. That is obviously a far different activity from that of a visit to a working prison and it has developed a specific literature linked to the so-called prison tourism. In the next paragraph I will deal with the visits to prison museums in their purely didactic aspects and as a tool for development and analysis of the emotions aroused by visits to prisons.

Prison tourism as a didactic tool

Prison tourism in museums is a practice that has been well developed in the international context, so much so that it has been the subject of extensive

---

17 This effect of the prison on the prisoner often has nothing to do with the critical review of the route that led him/her to the crime, but is due to the condition of inactivity of the inmate which leads them to externalise self-reflective activity which in life as a free person they perhaps would never have achieved. This condition also explains the singular phenomenon by which a lot of semi-literate prisoners start writing in prison and, in some cases, even become great writers.

18 This reaction, in particular, is demonstrated by some of the students in a very evident manner, when viewing a docufilm on the story of a group of life prisoners, so-called whole-life prisoners, in other words convicted of serious organised crime, interviewed after long spells of reclusion.

studies and has also been involved in the didactics of penal and prison law. The international literature on the subject has given precedence to analysis of how this tourism has influenced the construction of the prison reality and the collective imagination regarding the total institution. This is what Michelle Brown (2009) called "the culture of punishment".

However there is no lack of reflections on the impact that prison museums have produced when they have been visited for didactic purposes. The case presented here is quite singular, because the Museum we are talking about was set up by the Author of this essay, who is the same teacher that later organised the visits for didactic purposes for his own students. Therefore, while the teachers who have normally used this didactic tool have had to adapt to museum layouts built for mainly tourism-economic ends or as a celebration of the prison administration[19], the Museum of Prison Memory in Saluzzo was set up for purposes that, if not exclusively didactic, contain the elements for development in that sense. The final objective of the museum tour, in particular, was actually to offer elements for reflection on the history of the modern prison, from a Foucauldian perspective which enhances the elements of breaking away from the arsenal of pre-modern sentences and as a tool of the new disciplinary power which established itself with the modern industrial society[20]. This is evidently a critical approach that is well suited to introducing elements of reflection, as compared to the mainstream narrative on the history of the prison, which was called *whig*[21]. According to that narrative, prison should be seen, in a progressive vision of history, as a mode of penal execution which overcomes the pre-modern barbarism through philanthropic humanitarianism of a religious framework and the enlightened criticism of penal systems in absolute regimes (cf. E. Santoro, 2004, 3 and ss.). The didactic goal is therefore to bring out all the critical aspects of a total institution whose latent function is very different and more complex than that institutional mission which is, on the other hand, celebrated in the majority of museum institutions.

This goal is pursued through two communicating strategies which reinforce each other: the didactic tool of museum storytelling and the critical

---

19 These seem to be, in the opinion of researchers who have dealt with the subject, the main ends that have been characteristic of the layouts of these museums. For a classification of these cf. K. Walby, J. Piché (2015).

20 For a project that may to some extent be read from the perspective of the one in Saluzzo, a look should be taken at the project of the *Museo Penitenciario Argentino Antonio Ballvé* in Buenos Aires (cf. M. Welch, M. Macuare, 2011).

21 This interpretation about prison history plays a predominant rule in the existing museums of prison because of its attractiveness to the public (see A. Barton, A. Brown, 2015, 246).

reconstruction of the popular culture relating to prison and criminality.

From the first point of view, the museum tour was conceived with the exhibition mode of storytelling, a new way of conceiving the museum[22], which has revolutionised the traditional model, which saw it as a container of a certain number of works, objects, etc. suitably selected by so-called expert knowledge, according to hierarchies of relevance and of significance[23]. From the new perspective, museums are to be "understood no longer as mere containers holding, conserving and exhibiting objects, but as spaces for democratic, inclusive exchange for various categories of users. In the contemporary multi-cultural societies, museums are called on (...) to become centres of cultural elaboration *of* and *in* the local areas, a motor for development of a new culture of social inclusion and participation in the cultural life of society" (I. Salerno, 2013, 10). The museum becomes an interactive set of narrations, which concern the protagonists of the subject of the museum tour and call on the visitor to co-participate in this collective memory. At the centre of attention, there is no longer the work or object on display in itself, but rather the tale of the individuals who contributed to their production. In the museum of Saluzzo, the history of the prison is not reconstructed through the display of documents and objects, but the narratives of the protagonists of the history are brought back to life, both well-known protagonists and, especially, those forgotten by official history. In the case of the prison, this latter aspect bears enormous importance, since it makes it possible to elaborate a history of the prison "seen from the bottom"[24], which brings to light the critical aspects and the effective social functions, beyond the re-educational rhetoric.

There are various examples of how subjects linked to the history and to the present[25] of the prison may be dealt with, starting from the narrations that are held inside the museum. I will remind you of just a few here. The sub-

---

22 Compare to this model, often applied to museums of prison and criminal justice, the recent works by Hannah Thurston (2016; 2017).

23 Constituting, amongst other things, an effective device of power in relation to the institutional memory, as was clearly underlined by the Foucauldian analysis of the historian Eilean Hooper-Greenhill (2005).

24 And when I use this expression, I am not referring, as will be obvious, only to the persons imprisoned, but also to the category of the prison operators, in particular the prison officers, who are often, just as much as the inmates, forgotten and marginalised by the official history.

25 As is well known, the Foucauldian approach to history, "the history of the present", is precisely what sees the work of the historian not as an end in itself, but as that which makes it possible to understand current affairs, starting from the genealogy of the past, cf. for all H. L. Dreyfus, P. Rabinow, 1989, 143 ss. and D. Garland (2014). A. Barton, A. Brown (2015)

ject of suicide in prison, starting with the case of a prisoner who cooperated with justice and was "rewarded" by being given a job as an "archer"[26] inside the prison of Saluzzo, until one morning in August 1842 he abandoned his workplace and, as he was about to be arrested, shot himself in the head with a pistol in front of the clients of an inn. The subject of the conservative, bureaucratic juridical culture of the prison organisation, through the case of the first warden of the prison of Saluzzo, Giacomo Caorsi, discharged from his duties in 1834, because he put trust in the inmates and was opposed to corporal punishment for anyone who broke the rules, because that was humiliating the convict. The subject of the criminal career of marginal individuals through the tale of the brigand Francesco Delpero (1832-1858), who became a serial killer and "crime star" after having been imprisoned for the first time at 15 years of age in Saluzzo and condemned to 20 years of forced labour in the labor camps of Genoa, only because he laid his hands on a policeman. And we could go on.

Under the second profile, as was clearly observed by Alison Griffiths, "prison is a paradox: unknown to the vast majority and yet resolutely imagined through popular culture, what I called the *carceral imaginary*" (Id., 2016, 1). The *Museum of prison memory* reconstructs this imaginary through the narration of prison which the cinema, literature, painting, the theatre and music have produced. It is a question of dismantling the stereotypes and representations transmitted by the media and the various artistic forms, which have created an imaginary somewhat distant from what is the material reality of the total institution. This is not to claim an unlikely supremacy of the sociology of prison life in accessing empirical reality, but rather to reflect on the nature of social construction of processes of criminalization in their various stages. The artistic products that have influenced the prison imaginary and which are displayed in the *Museum of prison memory*, are of various kinds and come from various cultural levels. We can range from a worldwide icon of the prison imaginary, such as the painting *The Round of the Prisoners* by Vincent Van Gogh, the highest expression of the artistic view of the world of the disciplinary prison, down to the most commercial, second rate prison movie, which, however, contributes as a vehicle for stereotype images of prisoners and prison staff, mainly taken up by the US prison system[27]. From these cultural products, work can be done with

---

agree on this prospective about museums of prison.

26 These were the guards who had the task, in the prisons of the 1800s, of execute corporal punishment to inmates who had broken the internal rules. This enables us to deal with another subject related to prison, namely whether or not it is effectively a punishment that does not apply physical violence to the body of the convict.

27 As is well known, the collective imaginary of prison is nurtured to an over-abundant

the students on dismantling of stereotypes and the narrative frames, which enable us to bring out how the construction of the penal reality, which takes form in the popular culture, also involves the legal operators and strongly conditions the process of implementation of penal law. The stereotypes, in fact have an operational repercussion on the selectiveness of criminalisation processes. These works of reflection and dismantling of the collective imaginary are reconnected, amongst other things, to that thread of theory of law which Richard K. Sherwin (2007) called *Visual Legal Realism* and which dealt with how the visual popular culture influences the interpretation of the law and its application. Visual language, especially, has taken on great importance in the post-modern society, a language which education of the jurist normally does not take into account. The visits to the museum of Saluzzo and the subsequent discussions in class have therefore been very useful in developing sensitivity on the part of the students, which enables them to pick up the communicative aspects regarding in general the world of penalties. For example, in the museum, the last fifty years of the history of the prison in Saluzzo are recounted through the on-line archive of the Turin daily newspaper *La Stampa*[28]. This is an enormous archive of written texts and images, which brings back to the light items of local news, judicial trials, prison revolts for prisoners' rights and legislative reforms, all told in the popular language of the mass-media. The students are called on to analyse individual incidents of this history, with special reference to juridical aspects. This didactic approach allows us to focus on the juridical phenomenon in the wider context of the social and institutional history of an area and then analyse the juridical rules regarding the prison and their implementation, in the environment known by sociologists of law as living law.

Conclusions

How do we answer, then, our original question: is it useful and legitimate to organise didactic visits for students to prisons and prison museums? I add in the question of ethical legitimacy, inasmuch as some students have advanced a lot of perplexity concerning visits to prisons, since they might harm the dignity of the convict and his/her right to privacy in the context of

---

extent by images and narrations originating from American culture, which has long enjoyed hegemony in the environment of the blockbuster cinema. This predominance has also appeared, to a less evident extent, in narrative (prisoners turned famous writers, such as Edward Bunker and Jack Henry Abbott spring to mind).

28   http://www.lastampa.it/archivio-storico/index.jpp

daily detention. This is a very serious objection, which many researchers tend to underestimate. The "zoological garden" effect[29] is a distraction that is always present in the visits to prisons. The precautions to avoid this effect are therefore very important and, in my opinion, they are the same that must be followed to make the visits useful from the didactic point of view and I will talk about this shortly. Given that, it seems significant to me that the argument about safeguarding the privacy of inmates, at least in Italy, has never been raised by the prisoners themselves nor by the associations that protect their rights, but by the prison administration, which has never, in all these years, shown itself to be very zealous in guaranteeing other rights of convicts[30]. It is quite evident, then, that this is an instrumental exploitation of the privacy argument on their part, in order to prevent visitors coming into direct contact with persons closed up in the daily living spaces (habitable cells and corridors in the sections). It seems to be evident that it is not so much the inmates that are disturbed by the visits[31], as the staff that are worried that access to certain detention areas may endanger the construction of the predetermined institutional ceremony.

The main criticism that has been put forward against the visits to prison and to prison museums is that such visits do not represent the reality of prison and de-humanise the prisoners through genuine "screenplays" constructed ad hoc by the prison administration. The visitors, in this manner, take on a voyeuristic attitude towards the prison world and they are substantially reaffirmed in the stereotypes that the popular culture has built up around them. The undoubted suppression of the prisoners' right to privacy, caused by the visits, would then not be compensated for by the achievement of didactic goals, above all the elaboration of a critical view towards the total institution reality.

If we transfer these considerations to the Italian experience, which I have managed to experiment with, we have to note immediately that this screenplay on the part of the prison administration is much more informal and

---

29 This expression was used by Loîc Wacquant (2002), who also concluded his reflections with a favourable position on the visits to prison, or rather deploring the fact that this practice had declined over recent years.

30 It is sufficient to recall that it was the European Court of Human Rights in Strasbourg that reminded the Italian prison administration of its duty to observe the fundamental rights of the convict with its famous, so-called, Torreggiani sentence of 8 January 2013.

31 On the contrary, many of them show sincere satisfaction with the visits and consider them as a tool, even though limited, for communication towards the outside and to have their voices heard by young people who do not know prison. This attitude seems to be confirmed, at least partially, also by research in the U.S. which has dealt with the subject: cf. C. Minogue (2003 and 2009), more critical E. Dey (2009).

improvised on the spur of the moment by the individual prison. These characteristics make the screenplay rather fragile in masking the reality of the total institution; they are camouflage strategies that can be overridden, sometimes even with a simple request for information, as we saw in the visit to the brewery in the prison of Saluzzo. Furthermore, such strategies, in order to pursue the goal of presenting the prison as a place of employment and of re-education, require selection of prisoners who can speak to the visitors, which hardly corresponds to the stereotype of the violent individual who is dangerous and culturally crude. The paradoxical effect is therefore that the visitor-student is often struck by the humanity and depth of the thoughts and accounts heard during the visit and therefore comes out of it convinced that the representation of the popular culture relating to the prisoner is mostly over-simplistic.

The screenplays of the visits not only prove to be rather improvised, but they themselves may be subjected to study and reflection on the part of the student visitors. And here we get to the precautions that have to be taken by the teacher, in order to avoid the negative effects of the visits. The visits, in actual fact, must be preceded and, especially, followed up by explanatory lessons, which have the aim of introducing the student to the critical knowledge of the world of total institutions. The visitor-student, even before the visit, has to be put into a condition to be able to stay clear of the prejudices that the popular culture has instilled into him/her concerning the world of prison. His/her view must be that of the ethnographer and not that of the "tourist"[32], which the post-modern society has made so widespread. This will allow the student to pick up details and interpret what he/she sees in a very different way from how a visitor who is not equipped and is lacking in sociological and juridical knowledge of prison would see it. What will be decisive, however, is the discussion and re-elaboration following the visit led by the teacher involved. The theoretical concepts explained in class have a much greater impact on the student when it has been possible to test them before his/her own eyes. Once Goffman's concept of institutional ceremony has been described in class, the student can test in person how that concept takes form in the material context of the prison, as well as appreciating its nuances and the relational dynamics. Once the formal content of the principles and of the rules that regulate the detention punishment has been described in class, the student can appreciate how that content can sometimes be overturned by the dynamics of power of the prison. The visit to prison activates the student's emotive sphere, both through the human relationship, however limited, that can be initiated with detained persons and members of the staff,

---

32   The concept of "tourist gaze" is applied to the visits to prisons by Michelle Brown (2009, 97 ss.), but was also developed by John Richard Urry (1990).

and through the sensorial impression that the visitor gains from the set of images, sounds and odours that make up the context of prison. The same can be said when the visit is made to a prison museum, especially when, as in the case of the *Museum of prison memory* in Saluzzo, it is housed in ancient prison structures, with their disquieting, grim aspect, where there are also on display poor objects from the prison life, which evoke the daily deprivations and occasional violence suffered by the prisoners[33].

The capacity of the teacher for commenting after the visit on the emotive impressions absorbed by the students is that of bringing such impressions back to the rational, reflective sphere. The group discussion, if possible starting from written reports on the impressions gained from the visit, can be an excellent context in which to develop reflections and exchange opinions on what has been seen. The screenplay of the visit developed by the prison administration can be, in this manner, analysed in detail in its aspects of construction of prison reality, in order to bring out the cultural and organisational culture of the staff that produced it. The spectacle is no longer a screen that prevents appreciation of the underlying reality, but becomes itself a subject for study.

In conclusion, I believe it can be stated that the Turin experience of didactic visits to prisons and prison museums, as long as the precautions described in this essay are adopted, can represent a didactic tool that can become a fully effective part of so-called experiential learning. It is a set of didactic tools (legal clinic, training courses, operation of juridical information desks, moot courts etc.) which, when applied to teaching of criminal justice, has demonstrated undoubted benefits for students of law: increased sense of social responsibility of the role of jurist, greater connections between theoretical law teaching and its practical effects, increase in critical sense and in the knowledge of the methods with which the legal professions operate, greater capacities for identifying conceptual and practical links between the various subjects of law etc. (A.S. Burke, M.D. Bush, 2013; M. George et al., 2015). There is no reason why these positive didactic results may not be achieved also with visits to the prisons and the museums which "celebrate" their history.

---

33 As part of the visit to the Museum of Saluzzo, what always leaves a great impression on the students is the display of two strait jackets, used for "rebel" prisoners, at least up until the last decade of the last century. Compare to the concept of "atmosphere" created by museums of prison the interesting observations developed by J. Turner, K. Peters (2015).

References

Arford T., (2017), Touring Operational Carceral Facilities as a Pedagogical Tool: An Ethical Inquiry, in Wilson J.Z. et al., eds., *The Palgrave Handbook of Prison Tourism*. London & New York, Palgrave Macmillan, 925-946.

Bordt R., Lawler M.J. (2005), Teaching a Course on Prisons: A Design, Some Resources, and a Little Advice. *Journal of Criminal Justice Education, 16*(1), 180-192.

Brown M. (2009), *The Culture of Punishment. Prison, Society and Spectacle*. New York, New York University Press.

Burke A.S., Bush M.D. (2013), Service Learning and Criminal Justice: An Exploratory Study of Student Perceptions, *Educational Review, 65*(1), 56-69.

Calaway W. R. (2016), Going to Prison: The Effect of a Prison Tour on Student's Attitude Toward Punitiveness. *Journal of Criminal Justice Education, 27*(3), 432-448.

De Vito C. (2009), *Camosci e girachiavi. Storia del carcere in Italia*. Bari-Roma, Laterza.

Dey E. (2009), Prison tour as a research tool in the Golden Gulag. *Journal of Prisoners on Prison*, 18, 119-125.

Dreyfus H.L., Rabinow P. (1989), *La ricerca di Michel Foucault. Analitica della verità e storia del presente*. Firenze, Ponte alle Grazie.

George M., Lim H., Schannae L., Meadows R. (2015), Learning by Doing: Experiental Learning in Criminal Justice. *Journal of Criminal Justice Education, 26*(4), 471-492.

Goffman E. (1961), *Asylums. Essays on the Social Situation of Mental Patients and Other Inmates*, Doubleday and Company, New York.

Griffiths A. (2016), *Carceral Fantasies: Cinema and Prison in Early Twentieth-Century America*. New York, Columbia University Press.

Helfgott J.B. (2003), Prison Tour as a Pedagogical Tool in Undergraduate Criminal Justice Courses. *Corrections Compendium, 28*(1-2), 23-26.

Hooper Greenhill E. (2005), *I musei e la formazione del sapere. Le radici storiche, le pratiche del presente*, Torino, Einaudi.

Meisel J.S. (2008), The Ethics of Observing: Confronting the Harm of Experiential Learning. *Teaching Sociology, 36*(3), 196-210.

Miner-Romanoff K. (2014), Student Perceptions of Juvenile Offender Accounts in Criminal Justice Education, *American Journal of Criminal*

Justice, 39, 611-629.

Minogue C. (2003), Humans Rights and Life as an Attraction in a Correctional Theme Park. *Journal of Prisoners on Prison*, 12, 44-57.

Minogue C. (2009), The Engaged Specific Intellectual: Resisting Unethical Prison Tourism and the Hubris of the Objectifying Modality of the Universal Intellectual. *Journal of Prisoners on Prison*, 18, 129-142.

Nickoli A.M., Hendricks C., Hendricks J.E., Osgood E. (2003), Pop Culture Crime and Pedagogy. *Journal of Criminal Justice Education, 14*(1), 149-162.

Payne B.K., Sumter M., Sun I. (2003), Bringing the Field into the Criminal Justice Classroom: Field Trips, Ride-Alongs, and Guest Speakers. *Journal of Criminal Justice Education, 14*(2), 327-344.

Piché J., Walby K. (2010), Problematizing Carceral Tours. *British Journal of Criminology, 50*(3), 570-581.

Ridley L. (2014), No sustitute for the Real Thing: The Impact of Prison Based Work Experience on Students' Thinking about Imprisonment. *The Howard Journal, 53*(1), 16-30.

Salerno I. (2013), "Narrare" il patrimonio culturale. Approcci partecipativi per la valorizzazione di musei e territori, *Rivista di Scienza del Turismo, 4*(1-2), 9-25.

Santoro E. (2004), *Carcere e società liberale*. Torino, Giappichelli.

Sarzotti C. (2015), Storia dell'utopia carceraria e conservazione della memoria: il caso del Museo della memoria carceraria di Saluzzo e della rete museale sulla storia della penalità in Piemonte. Simonetta S., ed., *Utopia e carcere*, Napoli, Editoriale Scientifica, 125-140.

Sarzotti C., Siniscalchi G. (2013), eds., *eVisioni. Il carcere in pellicola, collage e graffiti*, Barletta, Ed. Linfattiva.

Sarzotti C. (2013), Il Museo della memoria carceraria della Castiglia di Saluzzo. *Antigone. Quadrimestrale di critica al sistema penale e penitenziario, 8*(3), 173-184.

Sautner K., Medina G. (2018), Using Storytelling to Establish Justice: How Civic Education Can Change Police Community Relations, *Journal of Museum Education, 43*(2), 114-125.

Sherwin K.R. (2007), A Manifesto for Visual Legal Realism. *Loyola of Los Angeles Law Review, 40*(2), 719-744.

Smith H.P., Meade B., Koons-Witt B.A. (2009), The Utility of the Correctional Tour: Student Perceptions and the Propensity for Academic Growth. *Academy of Criminal Justice Sciences, 20*(3), 292-310.

Smith H.P. (2013), Reinforcing Experiental Learning in Criminology: Definitions, Rationales, and Missed Opportunities Concerning Prison Tours in the United States. *Academy of Criminal Justice Sciences*, *24*(1), 50-67.

Stacer M.J., Eagleson R.C., Solinas-Saunders M. (2017), Exploring the Impact of Correctional Facility Tours on the Perceptions of Undergraduate Criminal Justice Students. *Journal of Criminal Justice Education*, *28*(4), 492-513.

Urry J. R. (1990), *The Tourist Gaze: Leisure and Travel in Contemporary Societies*, London, Sage.

Wacquant L. (2002), The Curious Eclipse of Prison Ethnography in the Age of Mass Incarceration. *Ethnography*, *3*(4), 371-397.

Walby K., Piché J. (2015), Making Meaning out of Punishment: Penitentiary, Prison, Jail, and Lock-up Museum in Canada, *Revue Canadienne de Criminologie et de Justice Pénale*, *57*(4), 475-502.

Welch M., Macuare M. (2011), Penal Tourism in Argentina: Bridging Foucauldian and neo-Durkheimian Perspectives. *Theoretical Criminology*, *15*(4), 401-425.

Wilson D., Spina R., Canaan J. (2011), In Praise of the Carceral Tour: Learning from the Grendon Experience. *The Howard Journal*, *50*(4), 343-355.

MAURIZIO VEGLIO

Chronicles of a Legal Scandal.
Migrant Detention and the Power of Education

> *"Education is once again a subversive force"*
> Richard Shaull
> Foreword to Paulo Freire, *Pedagogy of the Oppressed*

Introduction

As theatres of humiliation of human dignity and sites for legal and institutional suffering, migrant detention centres are an investigation field par excellence for legal clinics, despite being generally neglected by the public and academia. In a joint and concentric effort, students, lawyers, NGOs, lecturers and migrants have revealed how segregation threatens the fundamental rights of detainees: freedom, health, dignity, and safety. Legal clinics have transformed the nature of academic research into an inquiry on crime and punishment of non-citizens, offering a solid ground for a change. This paper reflects on the impact of clinical students' research on migrant detention in Turin (Italy).

Against the culture of silence

The doorway to the speakers' table, which faces a packed room, is lined up with a dozen plainclothes policemen. Their presence is conspicuous, as is the cumbersome police van blocking the entrance to the building[1]. The

---

1 The meeting was held in Turin on 7 December 2012 (https://docs.google.com/viewer?url=http%3A%2F%2Fold.asgi.it%2Fpublic%2Fparser_download%2Fsave%2F1_2012_cie_torino.pdf).

young researcher from HRMLC (Human Rights and Migration Law Clinic)[2] is presenting the outcome of the first-ever investigation into Turin's migrant detention centre[3]: accounts of forgotten voices, bodies, and dramas. Her tone is polite but determined; the list is detailed and merciless, as is the administrative praxis under question.

For several months, clinical students have been interviewing detainees over the phone and recording their grief. They had also applied for authorisation to access the centre and speak with its manager and police representatives, yet were never given an answer. Then quite unexpectedly two national newspapers[4] covered the investigation, and the suffering of migrants segregated in the Turin centre hit the headlines. Media hype and a few swift calls immediately opened the centre's gate to clinical students and ensured that there would be institutional recognition of the inquiry.

Today's event was meant to be a press conference, but local police officials, the centre's manager, as well as several judges and academics crowd around the speakers' table, and the audience is filled with civil society members, volunteers, and even a former detainee. Before joining HRMLC, the young researcher had never seen a single deportation order. After less than a year of training and practicing, investigating and reporting, she is publicly questioning State power before its representatives. And now she owns the floor.

"There is no such thing as a neutral education process. Education either functions as an instrument which is used to facilitate the integration of generations into the logic of the present system and bring about conformity to it, or it becomes the 'practice of freedom', the means by which men and women deal critically with reality and discover how to participate in the transformation of their world" (R. Shaull, 2005, p. 34).

Faced with the choice between conformity and critique, between domesticated reliance on the *logic of the present system* and joining the ranks of

2 Human Rights and Migration Law Clinic (HRMLC) is a legal clinical education program created in collaboration between the International University College of Turin, the Faculty of Law of the University of Turin and the University of Eastern Piedmont (http://www.iuctorino.it/studies/clinical-education/legal-clinics/#1455815004182-f7c06345-6b2b).

3 For the purpose of this work, migrant detention centres, C.P.R. (Centro di permanenza per i rimpatri) and C.I.E. (Centro di identificazione ed espulsione) are equivalent, identifying closed facilities in which migrants who have been issued a deportation order are detained awaiting identification and removal. Centres were established by Legislative Decree 25 July 1998, n. 286, "Unified text on provisions concerning immigration and norms on the condition of foreign citizens".

4 La Stampa, 3 November 2012; La Repubblica, 7 December 2012, https://torino.repubblica.it/cronaca/2012/12/07/news/costi_elevati_diritti_negati_una_fotografia_del_cie_di_torino-48267945/.

those committed to transformation, HRMLC has found its mission in investigating dark places of law to unveil hypocrisy and strive for change.

Focusing on the Turin centre, where migrants are detained after receiving a deportation order with a view to repatriation, students, lecturers, NGOs, lawyers, and migrants themselves have become members of a watchdog; indeed, HRMLC's educational paradigm in the context of detention is the *practice of freedom* for those who lost it[5].

The administrative detention of migrants for the sole purpose of deportation, which implies deprivation of freedom without any criminal record, entered the national scene back in 1998[6]. The controversial amendment – passed by a centre-left government – raised great concern among scholars, human rights activists, intellectuals and (few) politicians, in the view that administrative detention entails a *vulnus* to democratic values and a form of segregation deriving from the migrant status (Pepino & Caputo, 2004). Nothing short of a legal scandal. This detention regulation reveals severe marks of discrimination: the limitation of freedom is *reserved* to non-EU citizens who now come under the jurisdiction of lay judges (Justice of the Peace)[7] – a unique downgrade, since decisions on personal freedom are exclusively handled by full professional judges.

Furthermore, the legal ground for the detention of undocumented migrants is surprisingly fragile and fragmentary, often resorting to mere ministerial circulars where a law should be mandatory (Asgi, 2014). However, little attention has been devoted to migrant detention over past 15 years, with the result of silent acceptance and widespread ignorance[8].

Due to a Freireian *culture of silence*, the toxic cell of administrative detention – a modern-day civil death in the Western world – has reproduced and gained quiet consent from national public opinion, intoxicated before aware.

The academic world has been no exception: until recently, Italian universities have rarely offered any courses in immigration law or international protection, even though migrants and asylum seekers are often deemed the real actors of the 21st century. Quite astonishingly, reports and investigations on migrant detention centres have been largely absent from academic literature[9].

---

5 A similar effort was pursued by the Clinica Juridica per la Justicia Social from University of Valencia in 2015 (https://ojs.uv.es/index.php/clinicajuridica/article/view/6472/6264).

6 Artt. 13 and 14, Legislative Decree 25 July 1998, n. 286.

7 Justice of the Peace (Giudice di pace) is a non-specialist small-claims judge who is in charge of resolving minor cases or disputes under civil, administrative or criminal law.

8 Notable exceptions are a number of proactive NGOs, among which A buon diritto, Adif, Altrodiritto, Antigone, Asgi, Cild, LasciateCIEntrare, Medu, Melting Pot.

9 Interesting works came from the socio-legal field (see Campesi G., 2013; 2015. Pannarale

Borrowing Shaull's words: "Rather than being encouraged and equipped to know and respond to the concrete realities of their world", students "were kept "submerged" in a situation in which such critical awareness and response were practically impossible. And it became clear (…) that the whole educational system was one of the major instruments for the maintenance of this culture of silence" (2005: p. 30).

Do the (r)evolution

Upon receiving empirical accounts from lawyers and volunteers who had visited the facility, with full moral support from the Academic Board, HRMLC decided to defy the thunderous silence and embark on an unprecedented journey. The mission was to set up an independent agency that would inquire, according to scientific criteria, into life inside Turin's detention centre by bringing out the voices of detainees, those who suffer restriction on their own selves yet are very rarely considered subjects rather than objects (Freire, 2005: p. 88).

The active involvement of students, who realised that "the old, paternalistic teacher-student relationship is overcome" (Shaull, 2005: p. 32) and that "people educate each other through the mediation of the world" (ibidem), posited HRMLC as a new social actor and a (r)evolutionary factor, a place where knowledge is built through mutual effort from all stakeholders – the detained migrants now stand at the centre of the storytelling[10].

While fully aware of the illusory aspiration of neutrality, the researchers were rigorously committed to independency and transparency as they helped reveal the three-faced suffering permeating detention centres: institutional, judicial and human.

The extreme inefficiency of the Italian return system is no secret: according to ministerial figures, the average yearly rate of deportation amounts to roughly 50% of detainees (HRMLC, 2012: pp. 85-86), and official data on costs of pre-removal detention – even if presumably significant – are partial and inconsistent. The national detention centres' lack of transparency and closed-doors policy further aggravated the picture: civil society has been denied access to the detention sites and even the agreements implemented between the *Prefettura* (local representative of the Government) and the then oversight organisation (Italian Red Cross, in the case of Turin) remained classified.

L., 2014).

10 Along with them, interviews took place with lawyers, religious personnel and NGO staff who entered Turin's detention centre on a regular basis.

After a "long and emotionally draining task" (HRMLC, 2012: p. 91) – 9 months, 29 interviews and "hundreds of volunteer hours to research and produce" (*ibidem*) – HRMLC published the first in-depth report on living conditions inside Turin's detention centre. Conclusions drafted by the researchers are an eloquent example of independent academic investigation:

"I. Detainees do not take part in all extension hearings, despite the *Corte di Cassazione's*[11] rulings in cases number 4544/2010, 10290/2010, 13117/2011, 13767/2011, 9596/2012 and 10055/2012.

II. The current Italian legal aid guarantees do not include extra support for special cases where external consultants such as doctors or psychologists are needed to visit detainees or to write reports.

III. Full linguistic assistance is not granted as a matter of right throughout the whole legal procedure. While there are interpreters during the hearings, in the pre-trial stage the lack of professional interpretation can impede access to justice because it infringes on the opportunity to seek legal advice and express informed instructions to a lawyer.

IV. There is an urgent need to improve the relationship between the Italian authorities and the foreign authorities in Italy.

V. Evidence suggests that the military and police personnel inside Turin's CIE have not had sufficient training on European and international human rights law, or on working with culturally and linguistically diverse communities, asylum seekers and victims of torture and trauma.

VI. The *Giudice di Pace*[12] is an institution that has been built to deal with limited small claims matters. It is highly concerning that this forum is being used to decide cases involving personal freedom and liberty.

VII. In immigration matters where the liberty of a person is at stake, there is no provision for a merits-based appeal (…) of a validation hearing. The only manner in which a decision made by a *Giudice di Pace* in a validation hearing may be challenged is via an appeal to the *Corte di Cassazione* for judicial review. However, appellants to this Court generally face significant delays in having their case heard and time is clearly of the essence for appellants living in immigration detention.

VIII. Turin's *CIE* does not contain separate channels for consular visitors, lawyers, family members and other visitors, leading to a situation plagued with excessive waiting times and delays.

IX. The *Decreto Ministeriale 15 gennaio 2001* is being violated since Turin's detainees are not being given the amount of telephone credit that is prescribed by this legally binding ministerial decree. This is especially egregious since the telephone is frequently detainees' only means of accessing the world beyond the *CIE* and of keeping in touch with their loved ones.

---

11 Italian Supreme Court.

12 Justice of the Peace (see footnote #7).

X. Although there is much to be reformed about the Italian prison system itself, the overwhelming consensus among *CIE* detainees who have previously been in Italian prisons, is that prison is by far a better environment than *CIE*, which to a large extent goes to show how reprehensible Turin's *CIE* is.

XI. In order to avoid the possibility of extra *CIE* detention after jail, if a person is sentenced to prison and if that person faces a reasonable prospect of deportation, then the public authority should begin the identification procedure as soon as possible after criminal detention.

XII. There are insufficient activities and a lack of education and training opportunities inside Turin's *CIE*.

XIII. Often migrants are not taken to the *CIE* that is closest to where their friends and family reside. This can result in separation from children, family and friends who live in Italy, and it calls into question Italy's application of international and European legal principles on the right to family life and the best interests of the child.

XIV. There are endemic delays in providing medical assistance and medical examinations to detainees. The research indicates that this is a systemic problem caused by the procedure through which detainees access health care inside *CIE*.

XV. There is strong evidence to indicate the high misuse of psychotropic medication in Turin's *CIE*.

XVI. There are extremely worrying rates of self-harm by detainees inside Turin's *CIE*.

XVII. There is insufficient independent monitoring of immigration detention facilities in Italy and the current state of affairs does not meet Guideline IV(89) under the European Committee for the Prevention of Torture and Inhuman or Degrading Treatment or Punishment's CPT Standards" (HRMLC, 2012: pp. 91-93).

The dissemination of this report stirred public debate among scholars, universities, NGOs and civil society. HRMLC members organised and joined a number of conferences and public events, including presentation and distribution of their research to the then UN Special Rapporteur on the Human Rights of Migrants, François Crepeau (European University Institute, 2013).

Because they were "able to transform their lived experiences into knowledge and to use the already acquired knowledge as a process to unveil new knowledge" (Shaull, 2005: p. 19), students became means to denounce the pitiful situation of migrants inside detention centres: "Over the course of our report we have found that the human rights violations at Turin's CIE are so endemic and pervasive that they call into question the very existence of such structures and at the very least require a concerted attempt at re-examining the purpose and intended functions of the CIE and the wide gap between the former and reality. We will refrain from enunciating a final opinion on the same, except to say that even within our research group there was no consensus as to what steps should be taken in the future. However, we did unanimously agree that the present state of affairs is singularly untenable. The medical facilities inside Turin's CIE are woefully inadequate, families are torn apart and the legal safeguards are respected more in the breach. The people inside CIEs are not serving time due to criminal punishment. Rather, they languish in these structures owing to a systemic lack of support from their country of nationality and their country of residence and they are in many ways stuck in limbo: betwixt and between" (HRMLC, 2012: p. 93).

Candies for fools

Even more so than in prison, migrants held in detention centres experience State power in its most invasive and humiliating form. Detainees depend on their guards for every aspect of daily life, whether their position in the shaving waitlist, lighting a cigarette, or a doctor's appointment: as one of the volunteers told an HRMLC student, "They say that the key word inside CIE is «later»" (HRMLC, 2012: p. p. 44).

Like magnets of grief and marginalisation, detention centres often affect the health of migrants due to uncertainties about the future, ambiguous relationships with medical staff, inappropriate use of drugs – psychotropic medication and sleeping pills in particular – and temptation to self-harm. For those who refuse detention, the search for freedom often shifts from justice halls to their own bodies, which turn into forums for negotiating release by way of hunger strikes, lip sewing or object swallowing – deliberately becoming unfit for life inside the *camp* or getting hospitalised, and then trying to escape.

No surprise, then, if rage and despair periodically burn words, actions and mattresses inside detention centres, offering new ground for political manipulation, exploitation and false promises. It is no prison, according to purists. It is even worse, say the detainees. Similarly to the sphere of criminal justice, individuals who end up in detention centres are seldom the most dangerous or cunning offenders, but usually the weakest and most likely to suffer negative effects and deterioration.

The health policy of detention centres and its consequence on migrants' conditions was the core issue of "Emergency Exit. The protection of detainees' health in Turin's C.P.R.", the most recent investigatory research carried out by HRMLC on Turin's centre.

Extensive interviews with medical staff from the facility and from the nearby Martini Hospital[13] revealed a worrying degree of informality in the medical examinations assessing if the migrants are fit for life inside the camp, both on admittance and during the detention period. A similar situation was reported in the Martini Hospital, with uneven and impromptu practices being carried out on detainees, often due to the absence of interpreters or mediators.

The shortcomings affecting the migrant detention system also involve health protection: apart from general principles enshrined in international conventions and the Italian Constitution, the second layer of legislation is missing; the regulation of health protection inside detention centres is merely applied on an administrative basis (art. 3 of the Regulation laying down criteria for the organization and management of Centres for Identification and Expulsion, 2014). Furthermore, there are no statistical or monitoring obligations, confirming the status of these places as grey areas.

The exercise of fundamental rights of detainees is often hindered by bureaucratic obstacles due to the presence of multiple actors (management staff, social health workers, mediators, various branches of the armed forces and immigration officers), and to the high turnover of law enforcement staff assigned to the centre, most often without specific training on migrant detention. Consequently, simple requests for a medical examination or registration of an application for international protection can be delayed for days and even weeks.

The continuity of treatment is particularly at risk, not only for new arrivals from outside but also for those transferred from prison and already following medical programs.

Overall, the relationship between the detainees and the medical personnel, both at the centre and at the Martini Hospital, appears to be dominated by an identity clash – Us vs. Them – and the medical staff's presumption that detainees are often manipulating their requests for treatment.

An interview with one of the members of the medical staff who has been working in the centre for several years offered an eloquent testimony to the therapeutic and cultural deadlock that threatens the protection of the wellbeing of detainees (HRMLC, 2018).

In his view, detained migrants become "fragile", unable to live without "pills", responsible for self-injurious actions deemed "infantile", "immature" and even beneficiaries of a privileged service at the hospital – unlike "our elderly" – even at the expense of those "seriously ill". The patient's image becomes an identikit simulator, abuser, profiteer, locked in a dualism that denies room for mediation: the foreigner who cuts himself or swallows a mobile phone battery "fools" the doctor and deserves the blame, while the docile patient/detainee deserves a "candy".

---

13 The Martini Hospital is the regional health-care unit competent for detainees in need of treatment that cannot be provided inside Turin's detention centre.

Yet, the condition of serious affliction experienced by many detainees and the marginal chance of being released following a judicial decision not to validate or extend the detention – statistically less than 5% in Turin's centre (Lexilium, 2017: pp. 32 and 42) – expose foreigners to the temptation of self-harm. The last-ditch attempt to prevent deportation can transform one's body into a weapon of negotiation.

The failure of jurisdiction

The amount and the nature of the issues raised by the abovementioned investigations paved the way for the following question: are detention centres governed by a fair and effective jurisdiction? How can case law from the Justice of the Peace be assessed and made accessible to the public?

Again, the status quo was highly disappointing: despite dealing with personal freedom, decisions from the Justice of the Peace on migrant detention were neither deemed interesting for legal publications nor covered by academic literature.

As a result of this dearth, legal clinics from 5 universities decided to join forces and established the Monitoring Centre on Judicial Control of Migrants' Removal, to this day the only systematic observatory of national case law from the Justice of the Peace on third-country nationals' deportation from Italy (Lexilium, 2017).

Interestingly enough, it took no less than 13 months (and numerous denials) for HRMLC to obtain access to case law from the Justice of the Peace office in Turin, a unique indicator of how much independent investigation on judicial activity is needed in Italy. Data extracted from the Justice of the Peace's archives are alarming and confirm anecdotal accounts from lawyers, interpreters and migrants: half of validation hearings and 80% of extension hearings at Turin's detention centre last no longer than 5 minutes.[14] Several hearings held on the same day share the same opening and closing time. Files show that hearings are still held inside the centre instead of judges' offices – as dictated by constitutional guarantees – mainly on the ground of logistical issues in moving detainees.

The main causes for concern are the poor quality of judges' investigations and lawyers' defence, together with a lack of motivation that comes across in numerous decisions, many of which totally disregard the lawyers' arguments. In Turin's centre, third-country nationals are prevented from participating in extension hearings, notwithstanding the contrary position of

---

14   Figures refer to the first and last quarter of 2015.

the Italian Supreme Court, and judges regularly reject relevant objections. Hearing transcripts often show very limited activity from lawyers, many of whom (even in cases involving trusted lawyers) do not oppose the validation of the detention order. Roughly 60% of files highlight the lack of any defensive argument. Even when an adequate defence is provided, the quality of decisions remains unsatisfying, due to little, if any, legal reasoning and widespread omission of crucial aspects. The hearing transcript often displays a template form with pre-set motivations, and in 50% of cases the judge only adds a standard clause, without providing a specific reply to the lawyer's objections. The request for further investigation expressed by the detainee's lawyer is usually dismissed by the judge.

Figures from Turin's centre speak for themselves: the Justice of the Peace validates detention in 98% of cases, while the extension rate tops 97%. It should be recalled that these decisions can only be appealed before the Supreme Court, where lengthy procedures deny the right to an effective remedy.[15]

A disturbing and largely disregarded picture, which cries out for reform.

History is time filled with possibilities

The humiliation of human dignity suffered by migrants in Turin's detention centre has turned from being an anecdote to an evidence-based fact, as has the inadequacy of lay judges to decide upon personal freedom: "Preliminarily the defence lawyer requests the detainee to be allowed to the hearing room, so as to exercise his right to defence. The Justice of the Peace replies that the detainee is not here to defend himself, rather waiting to be identified"[16].

The HRMLC scope is deeply rooted in the rage against blatant violation of fundamental rights, otherwise doomed to oblivion. Its entire endeavour is to transform frustration into proposal, cynicism into hope, and minutes of everyday discrimination into chronicles of a legal scandal. "Human beings are not built in silence, but in word, in work, in action-reflection" (Freire, 2005: p. 88). Education must speak out.

---

15 According to 2017 official statistics from Italian Supreme Court, the average length of a civil procedure in Immigration Law is 12 months (http://www.cortedicassazione.it/corte-di-cassazione/it/statistiche_civile.page).

16 *"La difesa in via preliminare chiede che venga ammesso in aula il trattenuto in modo che possa esercitare il suo diritto di difesa. Il Giudice di Pace risponde che il trattenuto non è qua per difendersi ma in attesa di essere identificato"*, extension hearing transcript, Turin's detention centre, 29 October 2014.

References

ASGI (2014). *Appendice a Le modifiche al D. Lgs. 286/98 in materia di espulsioni e trattenimenti degli stranieri apportate dalla legge 30.10.2014, n. 161 (Legge europea 2013 bis)*. Retrieved from http://www.asgi.it/wp-content/uploads/2014/11/ASGI-Commento-modifiche-legge-n.-161-2014-22.11.2014.pdf.

Chomsky, N. (2008). Linguaggio e libertà, *Anarchismo*, Milano, Marco Tropea Editore, pp. 136-158.

European University Institute (2013, October 3). *A Consultation between the UN Special Rapporteur on the Human Rights of Migrants, Mr François Crepeau, Civil Society and Academia*. Retrieved from http://www.migrationpolicycentre.eu/event/the-management-of-the-external-borders-of-the-eu-and-its-impact-on-the-human-rights-of-migrants/.

Freire, P. (2005). *Pedagogy of the Oppressed*, 30th Anniversary ed., New York, Continuum.

HRMLC (2012, September). *Betwixt and Between: Turin's CIE. A Human Rights Investigation into Turin's Immigration Detention Centre*. Retrieved from http://www.meltingpot.org/IMG/pdf/CIE_Report_September2012.pdf.

HRMLC (2018). *Emergency Exit. The protection of detainees' health in Turin's C.P.R.* In press.

Lexilium (2017). *Observatory on the rulings of the justice of the peace on immigration: Office of the Justice of the Peace of Turin*. Retrieved from http://www.lexilium.it/wp-content/uploads/Rapporto-Torino-2016.pdf.

Pepino L., Caputo A. (2004, January 30). *Sulla detenzione amministrativa dei migranti*. Retrieved from https://www.meltingpot.org/Sulla-detenzione-amministrativa-dei-migranti.html#.W4nD4GT7RhA.

Regulation laying down criteria for the organization and management of Centres for Identification and Expulsion (2014). Retrieved from http://www.immigrazione.biz/4715.html.

Sanders, T.G. (1970). The Church in Latin America, *Foreign Affairs*, vol. XLVIII, n. 2.

Shaull, R. (2005). *Foreword to Pedagogy of the Oppressed*, 30th Anniversary ed., New York, Continuum.

ULRICH STEGE

How Clinical Legal Education is Crossing Borders?

Introduction

The last GAJE conference 2017 in Mexico was entitled *Breaking Down Walls: The Transformative Power of Justice Education*[1]. With this title, we wanted to face the recent political trend to establish/reinforce borders/frontiers within and around our societies. In addition, we wanted to emphasize the great potential transformative power, which is an inherent feature of education and which represents a great responsibility for all educators, especially for those acting in the field of law and justice.

In fact, nowadays a wide variety of different conceptions of the border as a physical and visible lines of separation between political, social and economic spaces, often charged with nationalistic energy, is again more and more *en vogue* in many regions/countries/societies worldwide. As an example, we only have to look to the policy responses of the EU and its Member States when it comes to migration and asylum.

It is in this context, that many new Clinical Legal Education (CLE) programmes in the Mediterranean context (North Africa and Europe) are in the project phase or have been created. Many of them seek to address with their students the consequences of borders, in its more classical geographical understanding, but also in its more broader interpretation, which also includes "political, historical, ethical, psychological and artistic implications and connotations and which can increasingly be seen as dynamic phenomenon that emerge, disappear, and re-emerge, as having a transitional character, as being internal zones of negotiation"[2].

---

1   See : https://www.gaje.org/conferences/9th-worldwide-conference/.

2   See the border concept developed by the 'Border Poetics' research group of the Artic University of Norway, http://borderpoetics.wikidot.com/border-concept.

By pointing out on some interesting examples related in particular to the field of human rights, migration and asylum, this chapter wants therefore to shed light on some of these CLE programmes or projects in the Mediterranean context, that in many ways seek to cross/overcome borders, for the benefit of those supported by them, but also for the benefit of the clinical students and the legal (and legal education) systems in place around them. By doing so, this chapter wants to demonstrate the potential transformative power of CLE, especially when it tries to *cross borders*.

But before coming to these single examples of CLE programmes, it will be important to recall some of the context elements, that provides the ground for these programmes to operate, such as the specific migration and asylum context, which is present on both sides of the Mediterranean Sea. In addition, it might be useful to clarify the CLE context present in Europe as well as on the other side of the Mediterranean Sea, which builds the systematic frame for these programmes/projects.

Setting the scene for the development of Clinical Legal Education: Migration and Asylum in the Mediterranean context

Within the European context, refugees and migrants crossing the Mediterranean Sea in order to find protection or simply a better life dominate intensively the public and political debate at least since 2015, when more than one million people made their way to the European off-shores (mainly in Greece and Italy). Although the numbers importantly decreased since then (2016: 363.425, 2017: 172.324, 2018: 116.647),[3] the debate has been significantly intensified and the language is getting harsher. This led to a general public, which takes position more and more against migrants and refugees. In Italy for example, in a study of end 2017, quasi 40% of Italians declared to fear that migrants are threatening their cultural and religious foundations.[4]

In addition, political decisions in the EU in the last years are intensifying the construction of a "Fortress Europe". "External borders controls", "Fight against irregular migration", "Hot-spots", "Detention and deportation of irregular migrants", "Common European Asylum System", "the Dublin-system", etc. became buzzwords of the political debate and drivers for a legal framework on asylum and migration in Europe, which on the one side still wants to provide shelter to persons, who arrive in Europe and who are in

---

3 See updated statistics provide by the UNHCR: https://data2.unhcr.org/en/situations/mediterranean.

4 See Demos Study from 2017 : http://www.demos.it/a01454.php.

need of protection, but which wants more and more on the other side to close the borders as much as possible in order to minimise the – as such perceived – "problem" of asylum and migration on the European soil.

Many of these policy responses raised and raise a number of legal, moral and ethical questions (Carens, 2013), which are constantly highlighted by international institutions (like UNHCR or the UN High Commissioner for Human Rights)[5], organisations, activists, NGOs, academics, lawyers and are in many ways also the basis of the work of so many law clinics active in Europe in the field of migration and asylum. Amongst those areas of intervention are items like support for a fair asylum procedure, fair hosting conditions, legal documents and the fight against unlawful detention and deportation of foreigners, unlawful *refoulements* on the external borders, etc.

Another buzzword in the recent years related to migration and asylum has been the "Externalisation of borders", where the EU in cooperation with selected African countries invest in the installation of border controls on the African soil, which should – as main effect – hinder refugees to cross the African continent until the Mediterranean Sea and further on to Europe. For this effect, the EU initiated different platforms for political cooperation on migration and asylum with African countries (e.g. Kharthoum Process[6], Rabat Process[7] etc.) and started numerous funding schemes[8] in order to support the implementation of these border controls and support of refugees far away from the European soil combined with the wish to encourage the economic development of these countries aiming at tackling as such one of the root causes of migrations flows.

However, in the funding envelope affected to migration within these EU funding schemes, most projects are designed to restrict and discourage irregular migration through migration containment and control etc. and only a meagre 3% of the budget is allocated to developing safe and regular routes. This "focus on short-term EU interests" has been often criticised as it "might jeopardize long term interests for African partners".[9] It is indeed difficult to

---

5 See the report of the UNHCR on "Better Protecting Refugees in the EU and Globally" (http://www.refworld.org/docid/58385d4e4.html), or the UNHCR position on relocation of asylum seekers (http://www.unhcr.org/news/briefing/2016/9/57d7bf1b4/unhcr-urges-european-states-increase-pledges-pace-expand-relocation-asylum.html); or the opinion of the UN High Commissioner for Human Rights on the situation of returned migrants in Lybia (https://www.ohchr.org/en/NewsEvents/Pages/DisplayNews.aspx?NewsID=22039).

6 See: https://www.khartoumprocess.net/about/the-khartoum-process.

7 See : https://www.rabat-process.org.

8 Such as the "EU Trust Fund for Africa" equipped with 4.1 Billion Euro, see: https://ec.europa.eu/trustfundforafrica/content/homepage_en.

9 See ECRE: https://www.ecre.org/trust-fund-for-africa-focus-on-short-term-eu-poli-

understand the long-term interest of the EU to support the re-establishment of border controls in an area of free movement such as – as an example – the area of Economic Community of West African States (ECOWAS, e.g. between countries like Mali and Niger). The ECOWAS area combines 15 States and is – in terms of territory – even bigger then the Schengen area. While the EU tries everything to safeguard its own free movement area (Schengen), which came under pressure within the so-called "refugee crisis", it is less understandable why the very main reasons in favour of it – mainly of economic nature– should not apply to the African free movement zones.

This becomes even more questionable given the context of colonial heritage, where the shape of the different African national states (and its borders – often only created "artificially" as outcome of the independence gained only recently in the second part of the last century) flows directly from its European colonialism.

In addition, it seems that the position of African countries regarding migration is fundamentally different to the actual engagements of the EU in Africa. EU seems determinate to avoid irregular migration and thus invest in limiting free movement flows in Africa, whilst the African Union (AU) attempts to increase the possibility of regular flows.[10]

The Clinical Legal Education movements in the Mediterranean context

Within such a general context on migration and asylum and given the number of legal, political, moral and ethical problems it creates, it seems without surprise, that CLE projects find enough ground for actions and activism in order to emerge. In fact, given the fact, that asylum seekers/refugees and migrants are often left in a sort of legal limbo and thus often are a particular vulnerable part of the society, and that the current legal systems and political will is often lacking to resource appropriate capacities and to provide suitable solutions for these communities, many law students and law teachers started to see the need to focus their activism in this area. Out of these engagements, many CLE projects all-over Europe (Bartoli, 2016), but also in some parts of Northern Africa (e.g. in particular in Morocco, but also in Egypt and to some

---

cies-jeopardizes-long-term-development-goals-of-african-partners/.

10   See AU position to Global Compact for Safe, Orderly and Regular Migration: https://au.int/sites/default/files/newsevents/workingdocuments/33023-wd-english_common_african_position_on_gcom.pdf; in addition, see the efforts the AU undertakes in order to create a African Free Movement Zone, adopted in early 2018: https://au.int/en/pressreleases/20180319/note-editors-african-union-will-enhance-free-movement-and-single-air.

extent also in Tunisia) [11] or the Middle East (e.g. Israel, Lebanon) (Wilson, 2017: p. 287) initiated or started to be engaged around this specific focus and it is indeed impressive to notice, how many new "Refugee Law/Migration Law/ Human Rights Law Clinics" projects have been created/initiated in Europe and around the Mediterranean Sea only in the last years.

As such, these CLE programme developments have also been directly influenced by the refugee/migrants protests in the recent years. Many of those protests, e.g. against the restriction on freedom of movements, received support by civil society organisations including law students/law teachers, who volunteered to support asylum seekers, refugees and migrants in their daily lives and bureaucratic struggles. From there it naturally evolved into providing more law-oriented forms of support and into the creation of more structured legal clinics for the benefit of asylum seekers/refugees and migrants.

Although often different and quite diverse (in terms of content and structure), most of these CLE projects share some common features. After a content (on refugee and migration law) and skills (linked to culture diversity and lawyering skills such as legal writing or interviewing) based preparation, the practical clinical activities engage law students in a variety of legal work, covering areas from direct pro bono legal advice to strategic litigation, research, advocacy and street law activities (Bartoli, 2016).

Some of them are working as in-house law clinics, where beneficiaries can access university facilities on specific office hours in order to receive supervised legal advice by law students. Other law clinics also receive their clients at the university settings, but their cases are pre-selected by associations following certain criteria (e.g. by selecting persons in a specific stage of the legal procedure, where professional legal advice is often not available due to the lack of public legal aid schemes). Another possibility to engage students in live client practise is to work closely with refugee associations (in a sort of externship law clinic model), where students would encounter their clients using the knowhow and the facilities of the local refugee association. In addition, more and more law clinics engage law students also in strategic litigation work to national or supranational courts, where through cooperation with refugee associations or specialized law firm, students are involved in the drafting/ filing of court applications. Some law clinics also involve students in research and awareness raising activities aiming at identifying and pointing out human rights violations. In these clinical projects, students become critical observers and investigators and are helping to identify and highlight problems of the law in practice (and their institutions). Good examples of these practical clinical research activities are the projects regarding the detention of migrants. Several

---

11   See the different CLE programmes in francophone countries at the website of the "Réseau des Cliniques Juridiques Francophone": https://www.cliniques-juridiques.org/.

legal clinics in different countries[12] have worked in their local context on the situation of migrants in detention. Finally, some law clinics engage in street law activities, where students are providing street law training sessions either to person working with beneficiaries or to beneficiaries directly and focusing on practical information on how to access certain rights.

All these programs are indeed good paradigms showing how the traditional legal education model can be challenged. Law students get a deeper knowledge as a result of the "learning by doing" pattern. In addition, they are elaborating on practical skills, like the capacity to interview a client in particular multi-cultural and often psychologically challenging settings. Furthermore, within the clinical settings, the students get individual feedback from peers, from specialized lawyers and sometimes even from non-legal professionals. Especially the later helps law students to reconsider well-established legal conceptions, fostering the effort to become a better and more aware professional, who interprets his/her role in the society in a critical, reflective, competent and social way and who are breaking down with the "Reproduction of hierarchy" (Kennedy, 1982). Furthermore, the law clinics engage students in general supervision/reflection sessions. These are crucial moments, where students share their experience and reflect on how legal institutions and practices operate and how they could be reformed to better meet the needs of the asylum seekers, refugees and migrants.

The experience of the many innovative and interesting CLE programs in Europe and around the Mediterranean Sea demonstrates on the one hand in many different ways the power, the usefulness and the success of this particular form of legal education. It proves to be an adequate tool to empower young professionals with competences and values, who are then able to confront the more and more globalised world and at the same time, to provide qualified and socially relevant support for communities in need.

However, we cannot yet maintain that clinical programs enjoy full acknowledgement everywhere in the Mediterranean context. Even if CLE programs are spreading out, we are still talking of a very small number of students able to get one of the rare places available within CLE programs. Also, many CLE programs face sustainability problems or are fighting for broader acceptance within law school curricula, and in that sense, their future might be problematic.

In comparison, it is certainly true, that the phenomenon of CLE developments in general, but also out of activism in favour of migrants and ref-

---

12 Such as the Law Clinic of the University of Valencia/Spain, the Migration Clinic of SciencesPo in Paris/France or the Human Rights and Migration Law Clinic in Turin/Italy (see the chapter of Maurizio Veglio with reference also to the "CPR/CIE project" of the HRMLC: http://www.iuctorino.it/cie-research-project/).

ugees, has been stronger in Europe then in North Africa. This has certainly to do with the fact, that the debate and struggles of refugees and migrants have been highly politicized and polarized in Europe, while it is often rather marginalized in the public debate in Northern African countries. In addition, as it is well described by Wilson[13] in his recent book, many legal education/legal systems in Africa are deeply dominated by the Africa's recent colonial heritage. Indeed, legal education in many African countries is still very much influenced and linked (in terms of content, legal framework, curricula, training materials, teachers etc.) to the systems developed by/in the former colonialist state, which often have been (e.g. in the case of France, Belgium or Spain etc.) rather famous for their traditional approach towards legal education and where indeed CLE still struggles to be institutionalised at a larger scale. Thus, the situation is still not yet comparable to a systematic introduction of CLE, as we can find it in countries like South Africa, Nigeria (Wilson, 2017: p. 205; McQuoid-Mason, 2013: pp. 7, Bloch, 2011) or Poland (Krasnicka, 2008; Ważyńska-Finck, 2018), but there are interesting developments, which certainly goes in the same direction.

Examples from the "border-line" of CLE:

Cooperation for the establishment of CLE programmes across the Mediterranean borders

Since many years, the development of CLE programmes in different parts of the World has been fuelled by structured or non-structured cooperation engagements by foreign grant giver and/or by more experienced clinicians or well-established CLE programmes across borders (Bloch, 2011; Genty, 2018; Wortham, 2006). This has been fundamental for the development and institutionalisation of legal clinics in many countries in Africa, such as South Africa or Nigeria (McQuoid-Mason, 2013: p.7), or Europe, such as in Poland (Ważyńska-Finck, 2018).

Many of this cooperation have their origin in the United States, where CLE is developed and institutionalised since long time already. Not only have US foundations invested a lot of resources in order to support the CLE movement in different parts of the world. The contribution of American clinicians in engaging personally with the development of CLE outside of the United States has certainly also been key for CLE programmes that we now see operating in certain parts of Africa or Europe. While US influence in the

---

13 Wilson, Richard J. Chapter on "Clinical Legal Education in Africa". 205-232 (Wilson, 2017).

international CLE movement is still very important, we can however recognise, that in the recent years cooperation regarding CLE is developing also directly within the Mediterranean context itself[14].

One interesting example of this is the cooperation for the establishment of a CLE programme at the Faculty of Law, Economic and Social Sciences of Rabat-Agdal of the Mohammed V University of Rabat in Morocco. Only two years after the establishment of its own CLE programme at the University of Bordeaux in 2013[15], the University of Bordeaux used its strong contacts and partnerships with the Mohammed V University of Rabat in Morocco in order to support the establishment of one of the first law clinics in Morocco. The law clinic in Rabat[16], which was founded in 2015 and is organized as an in-house clinic, open to legal questions from individuals/associations and small businesses mainly related to civil law and labour law. The structure of the law clinic is similar to the structure established in Bordeaux, which helps the exchange of experiences and know-how, but also the development of further collaborations. For example, it has been discussed that the master students of the recently founded joined Master *Droit des échanges euro-méditerranéens* (Master on the Euro-Mediterranean right of exchange), passing each of them a period in Rabat and in Bordeaux, would have access to the law clinics in each university, able to experience as such the practice of law in both continents and legal environments.

Another example of Mediterranean cooperation leading to the establishment of CLE programmes in Morocco is the recently established Law Clinic "Justice for All"[17] at the Faculty of Law, Economics and Social Sciences of the University of Hassan II in Mohammedia. Fundamental to this development seems the technical support received by Belgian NGO *ASF – Avocats Sans Frontières*, which is since several years already engaged in supporting access to justice initiatives such as law clinics in African countries like Morocco and Tunisia, and the Moroccan association "ADALA"[18] working for an equal access to justice in Morocco.

Looking in particular to the field of migration/asylum, we see in addition

---

14 In the context of this chapter, the focus is more on cooperation between Europe and mainly Maghreb states. There has been in the past also some important support amongst states in the Middle East and MENA countries, which created for example the conditions for the development of CLE programmes in Egypt o Lebanon. See Wilson, 2017, p. 287-300, chapter on "Clinical Legal Education in the Middle East".

15 See: http://www.cliniquedudroit.fr/.

16 See: https://www.cliniques-juridiques.org/cliniques/clinique-du-droit-de-rabat/.

17 See: https://www.asf.be/blog/2017/10/11/legal-clinic-justice-for-all/.

18 See: http://www.justicemaroc.org/.

several organisations/initiatives (such as UNHCR/the Refugee Law Reader[19] and the IIHL -International Institute of Humanitarian Law in San Remo[20]), which are trying to enhance the CLE development by organising training of trainers workshops targeting university professors, lawyers, members of NGOs from different Maghreb states[21]. The main aim of these trainings is to motivate and bring professors, lawyers and members of NGOs from this region in the position to integrate Refugee Law Courses (including a law clinic component) in professional trainings and law faculty curricula. At these trainings, law clinic models (such as the Human Rights and Migration Law Clinic in Turin – HRMLC[22]) have been exposed in order to provide an easy replicable model for their specific regional context.

In the same field of migration and asylum, another interesting initiative in Morocco is worth to be highlighted. Influenced from abroad, the Law Clinic "HIJRA"[23] has been created by a Morrocan researcher, M. Younous Arbaoui, who got familiarised with the concept of law clinics when he worked as Phd researcher at the Free University of Amsterdam. Stimulated by this experience, in 2015, he developed in Tangier the law clinic "HIJRA", which is structured as an association outside the university, but uses student/researcher' volunteers in order to provide legal support to asylum seekers. HIJRA now got expanded and operates also in Rabat and Agadir.

Similar are the engagements for the development of a CLE programme in Tunisia. Funded by the EU and with the support led initially in particular by the NGO *Terre d'Asile Tunisia* (and its *Maison du Droit et des Migrations*) and the local Association *Beity*[24] and again the Belgian NGO *ASF – Avocats Sans Frontières*[25], initiatives have been taken in order to open a CLE programme at the University of Tunis (Tunisia)[26]. Also here, different clinicians (from Europe as well) have been invited in order to provide informa-

---

19 See: http://www.refugeelawreader.org/en/.

20 See: http://iihl.org/.

21 Such as the training organised by the UNHCR/the Refugee Law Reader in Morocco in 2016 and in Tunisia in 2018 or the training workshop organised in San Remo/Turin in 2015.

22 The HRMLC was established in 2011 as cooperation between the Departments of Law of the Universities of Turin and Eastern Piedmont in Alessandria and the International University College of Turin (IUC), see: www.iuctorino.it or http://www.clinichelegali.unito.it/do/home.pl; see also Stege/Veglio 2018.

23 See http://hijraclinique.ma.

24 See: http://www.beity-tunisie.org.

25 See: https://www.asf.be/blog/2018/06/29/tunisia-making-access-to-justice-a-reality-for-all/.

26 See the "Clinique Juridique de la Faculté de Droit et des Sciences Politiques de Tunis" (http://www.fdspt.rnu.tn/clinique-juridique-0).

tion about CLE and to support the creation of a best-fit model for the local context.

As a result, we can certainly observe some important movements regarding the establishment of CLE programmes in the Maghreb region (in particular in Morocco[27]).

However, even if these cooperation efforts *over borders* start to see some interesting results, we are still far from a well-established CLE movement in North Africa. In fact, a number of problems have to be mentioned which serve as obstacles in this regard. First of all, some of the legal institutions (legal profession and law faculties in particular) are still very reluctant regarding CLE, as they are still very traditional and closed to innovation (especially if "imported" from the outside). Furthermore, funding from the outside (as it is the case in some of the Moroccan and Tunisian projects) can be a great facilitator to start a CLE project/programme. However, as showed by the example of Eastern Europe, external funding raises sustainability problems for the moment the funding is not available anymore (Genty, 2018: p. 30). As far as EU funding is concerned (as one of the main sources of funding available), it is also problematic that EU grants are frequently very specific project-based funding, where the establishment of a CLE programme often plays only a minor/side role. This takes often away the necessity of focus and flexibility, which *CLE pioneers* need to have in order to implement a new innovative legal teaching and support project in an environment, which is far too often still hostile to CLE.

Finally – again looking in particular to the field of migration and asylum – every effort in this area are not always seen positive in the eyes of the university/students/society. This has internal acceptance reasons regarding migrants, refugees and asylum seekers. But it also lies in the fact, that Europe tries to establish *cooperation* (and investing money) mainly for its own interest of closing borders. It would be certainly desirable that the MENA countries themselves, but also the support from the EU would much more also invest in active civil society responses in the area of human rights, migration and asylum, which is an important factor to create a peaceful confrontation for the challenges inherently created by all significant migration flows. CLE can be – as demonstrated in so many countries also in Africa (like in South Africa) – a meaningful tool in this regard as it provides important legal aid interventions in the area, but it also helps steadily creating better trained and socially aware legal professionals able to confront these challenges.

---

27 See the website of the francophone law clinic network (Réseau des Cliniques Juridiques Francophones) which plays an important role to provide moments to meet and to exchange amongst clinicians mainly from France and some other francophone countries: https://www.cliniques-juridiques.org/le-reseau/.

Law Clinics working on the border

Another interesting example of CLE operating on the borderline are the examples of Law Clinics projects, which are providing support for migrants/refugees directly on the border. The main example of this reality is the German NGO Refugee Law Clinic Abroad, which is now operating under the name "Equal Rights Beyond Borders"[28]. Founded out of a group of law students and graduates from several refugee law clinics in Germany, the NGO established as one of the first organisations a legal information helpdesk on the Greek island of Chios, where law students and graduates as volunteers for several weeks, coming from different law clinics in Europe, provide legal information to refugees who land on Chios. All legal volunteers are prepared by the NGO (related to EU and national asylum law as well as on how to provide legal information to refugees) and are supervised by practicing migration lawyers.

This example has recently been replicated by the Refugee Law Clinic in Berlin, where a legal helpdesk has been established by law clinic volunteers on the Greek Island of Samos[29].

Similar to these projects of law clinics going abroad, the HRMLC in Turin is trying to support – together with the Italian Association for Juridical Studies on Immigration (ASGI)[30] and the law clinic of the University of Genoa – a legal helpdesk in Ventimiglia, right on the French-Italian border, in order to overcome the lack of legal information for the hundreds of refugees getting continuously stuck on the border to France[31]. Although, this project has not yet achieved its full implementation, there is the idea to boost the law clinic involvement on remote places in Italy – such as Ventimiglia, but also other border places in Italy -, by using the potential of law clinic students volunteers, similar to the projects presented above by the German NGO in Greece.

All these projects have similar advantages and challenges. There is no doubt, that all these projects have been created (or are in the process of creation) because there is a present need of action and activism on the borders (internal and external EU borders) and they are therefore more driven by the social justice need, rather by the impact of such a project on legal education. However, there is something very interesting to notice. Clinical students are getting in touch with the project often by being involved in the more institutionalized CLE programme settings at the university before they then decide to continue either still

---

28 See: https://refugeelawclinicsabroad.org/ or https://www.equal-rights.org/.

29 See: https://www.rlc-berlin.org/samos.

30 ASGI is an Italian NGO of Lawyers working in the area of migration/asylum: see: https://www.asgi.it/.

31 See: https://www.theguardian.com/world/2018/jun/17/italy-ventimiglia-migrants-stuck-at-border-crisis-suffering.

before or even after graduation as volunteers. We can therefore observe, that these CLE projects are achieving – amongst other things – something critical for the development of future generations of legal professionals: to encourage students to find their self-driven motivations related to their professional contribution for social justice and the society (Wortham et al, 2012).

On the other side, these remote CLE projects are creating a series of challenges. There are logistical problems linked to the intervention far away from university settings, which creates problems of the full availability of trainers and supervisors able to intervene in the quality control of the legal service provision, but also on the educational/legal training aspect of the project. If the supervisors cannot be available continuously on the border, there might be models of remote supervisions (using also new technologies) that might cover these issues[32]. However, the main challenges will remain and there always will be the need to employ responses with flexibility and creativity (involving all parts of the process).

In addition, these remote CLE models open also a series of ethical/deontological questions. The fact that foreign students/graduates, trained in another EU country (as it is the case in Refugee Law Clinic projects in Greece), provide legal information to asylum seekers and refugees in another EU country, is creating some important questions. While law students in Germany are allowed to provide legal advice (under supervision) in Germany[33], they are not allowed to do so in Greece or in Italy (or in most other European country). Only qualified lawyers are allowed to provide legal services in these countries. Clinical students/volunteers are therefore allowed to provide *only* legal information (under the supervision of lawyers), which in practice, is a *dance on a very thin line* between an allowed and a forbidden legal intervention, which obviously is even more complicated, if the supervising lawyer is only supervising remotely.

But given the obvious need for legal support for refugees and asylum seekers on the borders, it would be desirable to continue and to boost suitable solutions in order to use the positive motivation of law students and graduate volunteers, but also to use their experience in order to find stable and more adequate responses to the emergency problems that Europe is creating itself on its internal and external borders.

---

32 As discussed at the South African Law Teachers Conference (SALTC) Conference July 2018 in Cape Town (SA), Lourens Grove & Ulrich Stege, "Remote legal clinics as a tool to enhance access to justice and law students capacities", see: http://www.lawatwork.uct.ac.za/sites/default/files/image_tool/images/251/Courses/SLTSA_List%20of%20Panels_3.pdf.

33 In 2008 the German legal advice law (the "Rechtsdienstleistungsgesetz") has been amended by opening the possibility for students to provide legal advice (not to represent a client before a court though) under supervision of a qualified lawyer.

CLE projects crossing the "border" of disciplines

Finally, there are more and more CLE projects[34], which wish to cross the traditional borders of law and provide the law clinic student with a much broader experience of the law in action. As a significant example, one could mention the Refugee Law Clinic of the HRMLC in Turin, where students work on real asylum law cases. In this context, clinical students – supervised directly by specialized lawyers – engage in the following activities: (1) meeting the asylum seekers, (2) scrutinizing the applicants' stories, (3) searching for all relevant case law and Country of Origin Information, (4) preparing legal memos containing the background story and an analysis of all relevant legal issues and (5) providing the asylum seekers with theoretical and practical information regarding their legal situation.

Aware of the need to broaden the competencies and abilities of students, the HRMLC enhanced its multidisciplinary approach in 2015 by starting cooperation with Turin University's Department of Anthropology. Supervised anthropology students support clinical students in interviewing asylum seekers and researching relevant Country of Origin Information.[35] This multidisciplinary approach proofed extremely successful in different means. Through the students' cooperation, law clinic students explore law in action also through the lenses of students from other disciplines, and investigate more completely in the myriad of legal and non-legal factors which influences the social, legal, political and economic arrangements in society. In addition, law clinic students are also learning from non-legal professionals, which helps them to reconsider well-established legal conceptions, fostering in them the necessary competences to become better and more aware professionals.

But not only the law students benefit from a multidisciplinary approach in CLE. Jovana Bogićević, an anthropology student, who took part at the Refugee Law Clinic in Turin in 2018, mentioned at her intervention at the 6th European Network for Clinical Legal Education (ENCLE) Conference[36] in Turin (Italy), that "the practical experience also for the students of the discipline such is anthropology is of immense importance as it gives them the opportunity to apply and to question the knowledge they learn at the University. Anthropology is a science that has traditionally trying to study and to understand the «Other». The work with the asylum seekers goes

---

34 See also the chapter above from Cecilia Blengino.

35 In cooperation with the team of Prof. Roberto Beneduce and Prof. Simona Taliani of the Department on Culture, Politics and Society ("Dipartimento Cultura, Politica e Società") of the University of Turin, see: http://www.didattica-cps.unito.it/do/docenti.pl/Show?_id=rbeneduc.

36 See: http://www.encle2018torino.unito.it/en/content/programme.

exactly in the same direction, except that now the «other» is coming to us".

In addition, she claims another interesting aspect of a benefit earning from such a multidisciplinary CLE project. As the asylum system is continuously evolving and changing, it would be important to consider the place of anthropology and other humanities within it. Bogićević claims that the asylum system and migration related policies in Europe would benefit from the implementation of anthropological knowledge and the experiences and struggles that students at the HRMLC had, could indeed be a very interesting tool to discuss the way, how this knowledge could find its systematic place within a continuously evolving asylum systems.

Conclusion

It is part of the fascination of CLE to be able to *cross borders* in so many ways. The above-mentioned cases are only some small examples of the potential of CLE programmes, based in the specific context of migration and asylum, and its transformative power for the beneficiaries, but also for the students and the society as a whole. Let's continue to enjoy the fascination of CLE crossing borders and to boost its full potential everywhere, for the benefit of future generations of socially more aware professionals and the society. In this regard, it will be important, that:

(1) CLE stabilize and increase and with it, the number of students who can participate. In this regard, it is important to note, that law clinics in the field of asylum and migration have proven to be interesting as it combines the potential to gather motivation amongst students and teachers with the evident need for social justice engagements.
(2) Universities should find adequate ways inside the academic settings structures and resources to keep and to encourage the engagement of faculty who run a CLE program. Academic recognition, but also regular and specific funding for clinical programs will be fundamental.
(3) The CLE networks and communities in the Mediterranean context should be strengthened. On-going collaboration amongst the CLE community is to our great mutual advantage.

References

Alemanno, Alberto & Khadar, Lamin (Eds.), "Reinventing Legal Education. How Clinical Education is Reforming the Teaching and Practice of Law in Europe". Cambridge: CUP, 2018.

Bartoli, Clelia. "Legal clinics in Europe: for a commitment of higher education in social justice", *Diritto & Questioni Pubbliche*, 2016: Special issue (http://www.dirittoequestionipubbliche.org/page/2016_nSE_Legal-clinics-in-Europe/DQ_2016_Legal-Clinics-in-Europe_specialissue.pdf)

Bloch, Frank. "The Global Clinical Movement: Educating Lawyers for Social Justice", Oxford: Oxford University Press, 2011

Carens, Joseph H. "The ethics of immigration". Oxford: Oxford University Press, 2013.

Genty, Philip M. "Reflections on US Involvement in the Promotion of Clinical Legal Education in Europe", 29-43 in A. Alemanno & L. Khadar (Eds.), *Reinventing Legal Education: How Clinical Education Is Reforming the Teaching and Practice of Law in Europe*. Cambridge: CUP 2018.

Krasnicka, Izabela, "Legal Education and Clinical Legal Education in Poland", *International Journal of Clinical Legal Education*, 12/2008 [accessible: http://www.northumbriajournals.co.uk/index.php/ijcle/article/viewFile/67/70]

McQuoid-Mason, David. "The History of Live Client Clinics in Africa", 7-15, *in* McQuoid-Mason, D. & Palmer, R. (Eds.), *African Law Clinician's Manual*, Durban: Institute of Professional Legal Training, 2013, [accessible: https://www.gaje.org/training-of-trainers-workshop-designing-models-of-social-justice-clinics/].

McQuoid-Mason, David & Ojukwu, Ernest & Mokundi Wachira, George. "Clinical Legal Education in Africa: Legal Education and Community Service", 23-36, in Bloch, F, *The Global Clinical Movement: Educating Lawyers for Social Justice,* Oxford: Oxford University Press, 2011

Kennedy, Duncan. "Legal Education and the Reproduction of Hierarchy", *Journal of Legal Education* 32 (1982): 591-615.

Stege, Ulrich & Veglio, Maurizio, "On the Front Line of the Migrant Crisis: The Human Rights and Migration Law Clinic (HRMLC) in Turin", 127-144, in A. Alemanno & L. Khadar (Eds.), *Reinventing Legal Education. How Clinical Education is Reforming the Teaching and Practice of Law in Europe*. Cambridge: CUP, 2018.

Ważyńska-Finck, Katarzyna. "Poland as the Success Story of Clinical Legal

Education in Central and Eastern Europe". 44-56, in A. Alemanno & L. Khadar (Eds.), *Reinventing Legal Education: How Clinical Education Is Reforming the Teaching and Practice of Law in Europe*. Cambridge: CUP 2018.

Wilson, Richard J., "The Global Evolution of Clinical Legal Education: More than a Method. Cambridge: CUP 2017.

Wortham, Leah, "Aiding Clinical Education Abroad: What Can Be Gained and The Learning Curve on How to Do So Effectively", 12 CLINICAL L. REV. 615 (2006).

Wortham, Leah & Klein, Catherine & Blaustone, Beryl, "Autonomy-Mastery-Purpose: Structuring Clinical Courses To Enhance These Critical Educational Goals", *International Journal of Clinical Legal Education*, Vol. 18, 2012 [accessible: http://www.northumbriajournals.co.uk/index. php/ijcle/article/view/2].

Notes of Contributors

Andres Gascon-Cuenca (andres.gascon@uv.es) is a postdoctoral researcher at the Human Rights Institute of the University of Valencia. His principal field of research is Human Rights, where he has concentrated on anti-discrimination law, racial profiling, hate speech regulations, minorities rights, among others. He is a member of the Legal Clinic for Social Justice of the University of Valencia since 2011, and now he is its Co-director. He has participated in several meetings and conferences as guest speaker, trainer of trainers and presenting panels altogether with colleagues from different universities. He has been a guest researcher at the University of Turin where he has collaborated with the Legal Clinic Prison and Rights I (March-May 2018). He is a member of the European Network of Clinical Legal Education (ENCLE) and the elected member representing Western Europe in the Global Alliance of Justice in Education (GAJE).

Cecilia Blengino (ceciliapiera.blengino@unito.it) is an assistant professor of Sociology of Law and Philosophy of Law at the Department of Law of the University of Torino. Her field of research mainly deals with sociology of criminal law, justice management, access to justice and clinical legal education. She wrote several publications in those areas. Since 2011 she has been involved in clinical legal education projects and she is now the director of both the Legal Clinic Prison and Rights I and the Human Trafficking Law Clinic at the University of Turin. She has participated in several ENCLE conferences in Olomouc (2014); Budapest (2015), Valencia (2017) and Turin (2018), cooperating with colleagues to organize presentations in the GAJE conferences in Turkey (2015) and in Mexico (2018). In 2017 she participated as lecturer in the course of Human Rights at the degree in Law in the University of Valencia.

Jose Garcia-Añon (jose.garcia@uv.es) is full professor of Legal Philosophy at the Department of Legal Philosophy and Politics of the Faculty of Law,

University of Valencia. He is a member of the Human Rights Institute at the same university and his main research area is Human Rights. He is specialized in anti-discrimination law, racial profiling, racial discrimination, multiculturalism, protection of minorities, access to justice, among others. He is one of the founding faculty of the Legal Clinic for Social Justice of the University of Valencia. He has been a guest professor at the University of Turin in the year 2015 where he has collaborated with the course of Sociology of Criminal Law and the Legal Clinic Prison and Rights.

Jose Antonio García-Sáez (J.Antonio.Garcia@uv.es) is full time professor at the Department of Philosophy of Law and researcher at the Human Rights Institute, University of Valencia. He has been a professor at the Autonomous University of Coahuila (México), where he has directed the Centre for Strategic Litigation and has coordinated several human rights clinics (2015-2016). Moreover, he has been a professor in the Philosophy of Law Area at the Autonomous University of Madrid (2017-2018).

Silvia Mondino (silvia.mondino@unito.it) holds a PhD in Sociology and Philosophy of Law. She is a postdoctoral researcher, at the Department of Law of the University of Torino. She partecipated to the GAJE conferences in Turkey (2015) and Mexico (2018) and to the ENCLE conferences in Budapest (2015) and Turin (2018).

Claudio Sarzotti (claudio.sarzotti@unito.it) is full Professor of Sociology of Law at the Department of Law of the University of Torino. He is specialized in Sociology of Criminal Law. He is the principal investigator of several empirical research projects as well as theoretical analyzes on both the justice and the penitentiary systems. He is involved in various innovative projects of legal education. He currently leads the Italian Association Diritto e Società and he is the President of the NGO Antigone Piemonte. He is also the Scientific Director of the Museum of Prison Memory in the city of Saluzzo.

Maurizio Veglio (maurizio.veglio@gmail.com) is a clinical faculty member at the International University College of Turin (IUC) and a lawyer, admitted to the Turin bar, specialising in immigration law. Since 2006 he has been a member of the Association for Legal Studies on Migration (ASGI), and he is working at the Turin's Human Rights and Migration Law Clinic (HRMLC), where he supervised the *Betwixt and Between: Turin's CIE* report, on detention's condition inside local deportation centre, the establishment of the Refugee Law Clinic (RLC), supporting asylum seekers, and the launching of the Monitoring Centre on Judicial Control of Migrants' Removal, Lexilium. Beside lecturing duties and several training programs, he is author of articles and contributions on magazines and websites. He recently edited the book *L'attualità del male. La Libia dei lager è verità processuale,* Edizioni SEB27, 2018.

Ulrich Stege (ustege@iuctorino.it) is an International University College of Turin (IUC) Faculty Member, Director of the IUC Clinic Legal Education Program. In addition, until recently, he has been Lecturer at the Law Clinic of the University of Pretoria (South Africa). He studied law in Germany, France and Belgium. Beside his role at the IUC, he is practicing as a qualified lawyer in Italy and Germany (admitted to the Bar in Germany and Italy). He acted as speaker, expert and trainer in numerous conferences, international expert groups and Training of Trainers (mainly related to European Law, Asylum and Immigration Law and Clinical Legal Education). He is founding member and Executive Secretary of ENCLE, Steering Committee member of GAJE and member of ASGI and the Migration Law Network (Germany – www.netzwerk- migrationsrecht.de).

QUADERNI DEL DIPARTIMENTO DI GIURISPRUDENZA DELL'UNIVERSITÀ DI TORINO

www.ingramcontent.com/pod-product-compliance
Lightning Source LLC
Chambersburg PA
CBHW061818210326
41599CB00034B/7035